Who the Hell is Betty Friedan?

Who the Hell is Betty Friedan?

And what are her theories all about?

Betty Londergan

First published in Great Britain in 2020 by
Bowden & Brazil Ltd
Woolverstone, Suffolk, UK.

ISBN 978-1-9999492-7-3

To find out more about other books and authors in this series,
visit www.whothehellis.co.uk

Contents

Introduction

Like so many feminists before her, Betty Friedan has often been overlooked, underappreciated and misunderstood in the annals of history. Her legacy has been tainted with all the usual tropes about powerful women who dare to lead: she wasn't pretty enough, she was too intellectual, she talked too much, she was too sure of herself, she didn't fade away even in her old age. Yet what can never be denied is Friedan's unique ability to inspire, motivate and mobilize millions of women to challenge the status quo – with her wise words and ambitious action.

Loud, volatile, brilliant, incisive, charismatic and courageous, Friedan is largely credited with setting off the Second Wave of feminism with the publication of her book, *The Feminine Mystique*, in 1963. In this tome, she identified 'the problem that has no name' as the oppressive ideology that conflated femininity with subservience while insisting there is no greater happiness or fulfillment for women than to devote themselves completely to the care of their husbands, fathers, brothers and/or children. In other words, anyone but themselves. By 1970, *The Feminine Mystique* had sold 1.5 million copies, deftly undermined that ideology, and taken pride of place within the women's liberation movement, by then in full bloom.

This seminal blockbuster of a book was described by *Future Shock* author Alvin Toffler as having 'pulled the trigger on history'. By tracing the ways in which 'the problem with no name' was framed and discussed, and allowing women to speak the truth about their own lives, Friedan was able to show precisely how societal forces shape and dictate norms. She also elucidated the ways in which those forces led women to conform, even when they were unaware they were being manipulated. Friedan has been credited with being one of the first to explicitly reveal how ideology (in this case patriarchy) may operate in a way that is decentralized, ubiquitous, and historically changeable (Eagle 2018); even when it superficially alters, it never loses its power to control.

The Feminine Mystique catapulted Friedan onto the world stage, where she worked for the next 40 years to change everyday life and possibilities for women around the globe. In the women's movement of the late 20th century, she was ubiquitous and indefatigable. Having kick-started the Second Wave with the wake-up call of *The Feminine Mystique*, she turned her attention to activism, insisting that thinking differently wasn't enough. There were changes that needed to be made. In 1966, she co-founded the National Organization for Women, dedicated to passing the Equal Rights Amendment, securing reproductive rights for women, and ensuring that women had full equality in education, at work, and in the justice system. In 1969, she co-founded the National Association for the Repeal of Abortion Laws (NARAL) to advocate for a woman's right to an abortion, and in August the following year organized the largest women's march to date, celebrating the 50th anniversary of the ratification of the 19th Amendment, which granted American women the right to vote.

Within six years she had co-founded the National Women's Political Caucus (NWPC); met with Pope Paul VI to discuss the Catholic Church, women and society; convened the first International Feminist Conference; and organized an 894-resolution 'World Plan of Action'. In 1976 she published *It Changed My Life*, a compilation of speeches, editorials and columns, and in 1981, *The Second Stage*, a somewhat contradictory yet prescient book positing the need for flexitime working, maternity and paternity leave, and guaranteed child care for the evolving (and more equal) American family. At the age of 72, she published *The Fountain of Age*, encouraging people to consider old age as a time of learning, wisdom and new opportunities for personal growth.

In 1997 her 'New Paradigm' seminars (given at the Woodrow Wilson International Center for Scholars) were collected into the book *Beyond Gender*, calling for nothing less than 'a new paradigm of women, men, and community'. In 2000, she published her autobiography, *Life So Far*, because she felt that 'the unauthorized biographies they would publish about me would be... false, mistaken, sensational and trivializing'. Friedan was not about to let anyone else speak for her, particularly since deconstructing the fabricated image of 'woman' and letting women speak for themselves had been her life's work. Not surprisingly, she picked up her pen 'to put down my life the way I experienced it'.

Friedan's place in the pantheon of feminist leaders of the 20th century is indisputable, but she was a woman of many contradictions. Egotistical and self-involved, she was also a champion of justice and equality. Although her most famous book focused almost exclusively on white, affluent suburban women, who were paralyzed by depression despite seeming 'to have it all', she spent decades of her life working internationally to improve the lives of women in developing countries and to challenge income inequality around the globe. She was notoriously difficult to work with, blithely took advantage of the women who worked alongside her, and quickly lost leadership positions in the very organizations she founded, yet she adapted, moved on, and continued the work. Even in her marriage, this feminist trailblazer had a history of violence, heavy drinking and bad behaviour, yet her children (and even ex-husband) remained in her life until the end.

By any measure, Betty Friedan was a uniquely memorable individual who made big things happen. We could use her passionate leadership today.

1. Friedan's Life Story

Betty Friedan was incredibly smart, proudly female, and convinced she was not in any way beautiful. This trifecta of attributes would inform almost every aspect of her life and, bolstered by her tremendous drive and charisma, would lead her to almost single- handedly instigate the Second Wave of feminism around the world.

Born on 4 February 1921 to affluent Jewish parents in the staunchly Midwestern city of Peoria, Illinois, Bettye Goldstein (she later dropped the pretentious 'e') was the first of three children. Her younger sister Amy was a mere 18 months younger than Betty and a beauty; her robust brother Harry was born three years later. In her own words, Betty was not a golden child: 'All in all, I have not been well endowed physically, neither with health nor with beauty' (Friedan 1938, quoted in Hennessee 1999). Her lungs were feeble – she suffered all her life from bronchitis and debilitating bouts of asthma so severe they required hospitalization. Her teeth were crooked. Her legs were bowed, requiring her to wear iron braces for three painful years as a child. Her vision was so bad she could barely see out of one eye and she wore glasses nearly all her life. And then there was her despised nose – a big, prominent gift from her Russian immigrant father.

Meet the Parents

Betty's father, Harry Goldstein, began his working life in hardscrabble America, selling collar-buttons in the street at age 13. 14 years later he had worked his way up to owning the Goldstein Jewelry Company, 'the Tiffany of Peoria' as Betty liked to call it. As a young widower, Harry met beautiful, petite, well-educated Miriam Horwitz, the only child of a prominent Peoria doctor, and over her parents' objections (Harry was smart but uneducated and 18 years older than Miriam), the couple married in 1920.

The Goldsteins were affluent and prominent in Peoria society, but they still could not break the barrier of anti-Semitism that pervaded every aspect of the community. Even the ritzy Peoria Country Club was restricted, and no amount of money could buy a place for Jews in the social hierarchy of the town.

Nevertheless, the family prospered and Betty's upbringing was both privileged and pampered. However, the ostracism she suffered as a Jewish girl, coupled with her exceptionally high IQ (180) and rebellious nature, meant that she was unlikely to have a carefree childhood, particularly in 1930s Midwestern America.

From the beginning, Betty's life was a battle between her ferocious intellect and her towering need for approval – a struggle first made manifest in her rocky relationship with her mother. Miriam Goldstein was an elegant, accomplished, fashionable society matron who loved to dress up, entertain in her huge brick home on the Peoria bluffs, and supervise the family's nursemaid, cook and butler-chauffeur. While Betty was unabashedly her father's favourite, for her intelligence and passion, she and her mother butted heads vociferously and tirelessly. 'Nothing I ever did was right, ever satisfied her,' Betty claimed (Friedan 2000).

In the 1930s, the Depression hit America hard, and Harry's jewellery business struggled to stay afloat. Money became a major issue in the Goldstein marriage. With an immigrant's constant insecurity, Harry fought to keep appearances up and the family's expenses down. Miriam, with an affluent only-child's sense of entitlement, spent freely behind her husband's back and indulged her shopping and gambling whims. 'All three children would remember their father's suffering, his anxiety, his battle to generate the finances that would support the Goldstein lifestyle' (Cohen 1988).

However, Betty also remembered his anger, saying in an interview that her mother 'was always...building up huge charge accounts, trying to get out of the hole by gambling and then losing and having to admit all to my father, who had a terrible temper' (Antler 1998). Wracked by financial stress, Harry developed hypertension and heart trouble, so that eventually he had to retreat to Florida every winter. Alone in Peoria, Miriam took over running the family business every winter, which she did with ease and some satisfaction, becoming noticeably happier and physically much healthier (her chronic colitis disappeared completely).

Although Miriam had loved her work as the society editor of the local paper in her early 20s, she quit her job when she became pregnant with Betty and focused her considerable energy on her social position and the children. Researcher Marcia Cohen notes that Betty would eventually 'see her mother's "impotent rage" in feminist terms, a simmering frustration...for women who didn't have any power outside the family' (Cohen 1988). In her autobiography Friedan says that:

> *'I never gave much thought then to how the rigid cold narrowness of Peoria, the anti-Semitism, the discouragement of anything different, the narrow possibilities for the use of intelligence, creativity, adventurousness, must have affected my mother, growing up in Peoria.'* (Friedan 2000)

But that empathetic adult perspective eluded the angry and rebellious adolescent Betty.

Opulence, fashion and beauty meant the world to Miriam, who was outraged and embarrassed by Betty's sloppy grooming, careless hygiene and large nose. Miriam took the facial appendage as an almost personal affront, which she incessantly but unsuccessfully petitioned Betty to surgically 'fix'. It didn't help matters that sister Amy was lovely, graceful, neat and effortlessly popular. Betty's response to her role as the ugly duckling in the family was to fire back at Miriam with no restraint. If she was going to be called ugly, she'd revel in her matted hair and rumpled clothes. If she were thought sloppy, she'd keep her room in utter chaos. Betty showed withering contempt for Miriam's extravagant spending, love of fashion, and vacuous lifestyle and would later blame her mother for many of her own emotional problems and ungovernable temper. 'The rage that dependency bred in our mothers, exploding in us, was sometimes too awful to admit...' (Friedan 1976). It was a feud that would last a lifetime; Betty only let go of 'that love-hate that never dies' (Friedan 1993) in the final years of her mother's life.

Despite the conflict with her mother, Betty's elementary and junior high school years were filled with friends and activities.

She founded club after club, including the Baddy-Baddy Club, whose members exasperated teachers with acts of mischief, and the Just for Fun club, with organized Friday night get-togethers of record playing and kissing games. In eighth grade, Betty began to write for the school newspaper, acted in productions with the local children's theatre, and lost herself in a barrage of books which she read obsessively. 'The only punishment that worked was forbidding me to read for a day' (Friedan 2000).

It was only when she entered high school that Betty's confidence slipped and she felt herself an outcast in that landscape of pretty, popular, decidedly non-Jewish girls, each bedecked in festive sorority pledge ribbons. The high school sorority that ruled the roost over Peoria's teenagers rejected Betty's application to become a member:

> *'Entering high school, the other girls and boys who lived on the West Bluff, which was the nice part of town then, were rushed for sororities and fraternities. No Jewish kids were ever invited to join those sororities or fraternities, which ran high school social life in Peoria.'* (Friedan 2000)

In addition, Betty's school became so overcrowded that it split each year into morning and evening shifts, and Betty found herself the only one among her friends to attend school in the afternoons. Coupled with her rejection from the sororities, Betty remembered the loneliness of seeing

> *'the others...pass me, in their souped-up jalopies, on the way to Hunt's, the drive-in hamburger stand at the foot*

> *of Farmington Road, for Cokes or root beer floats, hot dogs or hamburgers, and they would be shouting or laughing and maybe not even wave at me.'* (Friedan 2000)

She took to going to the cemetery behind her house and sitting on a gravestone reading poetry, 'pretending I was Emily Dickinson'. School had been 'heaven' up to the age of 13, because 'it had been such a relief to be good at something, instead of a mess, clumsy, inadequate, bad, naughty, ugly, as my mother made me feel at home, no matter what I did', but high school was torturous in the early years. Betty saw that her brother somehow gained a higher level of acceptance and in fact he continued to live in Peoria his entire adult life. 'He could go home again', she realized, but 'I couldn't. My ostracism by my high school classmates was too painful' (Friedan 2000).

Betty decided that if she couldn't join those classmates, she'd beat them. One afternoon, walking alone as a car full of happy boys and girls once again drove past her without a backward glance, she said to herself, 'They may not like me, but they are going to have to look up to me'. Contemplating this vow as a mature woman, Friedan found that she distrusted its motivation, and felt it tarnished her, especially given the 'larger visions driving me now'. And yet that teenaged moment of epiphany shored up her determination to make new friends and follow her own path.

With her intention made, Betty immersed herself in every school society that offered an opportunity to shine: the newspaper, yearbook, a new literary magazine *Tide* (which she founded), French Club, Cue Club, Honour Society, Social Science Club, Debate Club and of course, the Drama Club. And shine she did.

At her high school graduation in June 1938 she was one of six valedictorians, admitted to Vassar, Radcliffe, Stanford, Smith, and University of Chicago. In her autobiography *Life So Far*, Friedan says that she wanted to go to Chicago, to study the innovative curriculum put together by Robert Hutchins, 'but Chicago was too close to home, not far enough from Peoria. I knew, without saying so, that I had to get out of Peoria and that I wouldn't come back'. She acquiesced to her mother's vicarious preference for Smith, which Miriam herself had wanted desperately to attend. It would be a fortuitous and defining choice.

College Days

Smith College in Northampton, Massachusetts is an historic women's college with a sterling reputation for academic rigour and high expectations of its graduates. Friedan described herself at this age as a 'loner', with a 'shell around me built up by the sorority girls' rejection...too self-consciously inadequate to make friends easily' (Friedan 2000). Yet she adored the heady intellectual milieu – writing reams of poetry, easily acing her courses, taking on the editorship of Smith's weekly paper and its literary magazine, and eventually settling on a major in psychology. At the time, she said, she was not a feminist, and 'only knew of suffragettes, with my new Freudian sophistication, as neurotic spinsters suffering from penis envy' (Friedan 2000). This was a view that would profoundly change during her time spent researching for *The Feminine Mystique* (see Chapter 4).

At Smith, Betty eventually found good friends, and finally 'got over that terrible self- consciousness about being different' (Friedan 2000). She also hit her stride as an activist and change-maker, using the bullhorn of the paper to protest against fascism abroad, against the secret societies of the college, and most importantly, to advocate for America's fledgling labour movement. 'Everybody knew her not only as Betty "the psychology brain", but as Betty the outspoken patriot, the throaty social conscience, who argued, always, for justice, for the poor, for the disadvantaged' (Cohen 1988).

Caught up in Marxist philosophy that was flowering in America in the 1940s, Betty published stories titled, 'The Right to Organize', 'Learning the Score' and 'Let the Laughter Cease'. She also passionately supported the maids' strike at Smith (an irony since her own room, which the maids cleaned, was always a mess). She earned countless literary and scholarship prizes, served on the Activities Board, the Psychology Club, the Phoenix Club and penned a senior thesis with her professor Harold Israel that critiqued B.F. Skinner's behaviourist theory and earned her a coveted graduate fellowship to University of California at Berkeley. When she graduated Sigma Xi (the Phi Beta Kappa for the sciences) in June 1942, Smith's president told Miriam and Harry, 'Betty has the most outstanding record of any student ever matriculated at Smith' (Cohen 1988).

> *However, in her most anxious moments Betty's weak lungs were beginning to fail her. She was hospitalized by asthma attacks at the end of her freshman year, for several weeks in the spring of her sophomore year, and during her senior honours exam. Upon her graduation (and throughout her life), existential dread and panic about the future manifested itself in brutal bouts of asthma that sent her to bed or to the hospital. This*

> *confident and strident scholar wrote later that at the point of graduation, 'I felt the future closing in – and I could not see myself in it at all. I had no image of myself stretching beyond college'* (Friedan 1963).

Boys, she realized, were always asked what they wanted to be when they grew up, but nobody asked her the same question. Girls in general were told, 'You're a pretty little girl, you'll be a mommy like your mommy'. But Betty couldn't see any part of that equation as relevant to her situation: 'I wasn't a pretty little girl, and the one thing in the world I didn't want to be was a mommy like my mommy... But what other kind of woman was there to be?' (Friedan 2000). This puzzle was later to feed into Friedan's seminal work to illuminate the lives of millions of women who were immobilized by a similar deluge of self-doubt.

From PhD to NYC

Luckily, life has a way of sweeping aside post-graduation paralysis. Betty went out to Berkeley and dazzled the psychology department of the university with her intelligence. But at the end of her first year, when offered the coveted $1,000 Abraham Rosenberg Research Fellowship that could support her through the completion of her PhD, she decided that to intensely focus on her career and scholastic achievement would prevent her from ever getting married and having children. '...with all the brilliance, I saw myself becoming the old maid college teacher...' she later explained (Horowitz 2000). That was a future that terrified her.

Instead of accepting the fellowship, she abandoned psychology and moved to New York City to begin working as a reporter for the Federated Press, a small, progressive newspaper agency that sent left-wing and union publications across the country stories focused on the contentious battles between business and labour. She hung out with an eclectic group of college friends, pacifists, Communists, socialists, blacks and working class folk in the city bars of Greenwich Village and on the beaches of Fire Island. It was the 1940s version of 'Sex in the City': late nights at the office, rough-and-tumble races to land a good story, ill-advised love affairs with married men, and lots and lots of drinking.

She also accompanied at least a few Smith friends to get an abortion, an illegal and criminal act at the time. 'Betty was the one they asked for help. She was the worldly one, the most radical among them, the one who...knew how to find out things that ordinary people did not' (Hennessee 1999). Friedan vividly remembered every frightening detail, even years later:

> *'I myself never had an abortion, though I personally accompanied several of these friends to scary, butchery back rooms, and shared their fear and distrust of the shifty, oily, illegal operators, and sat outside the room and heard the screams and wondered what I'd do if they died, and got them into the taxis afterward.'* (Friedan 1976)

Many years later, in 1966, when writing the official Statement of Purpose for NOW (National Organization for Women), she insisted on including a demand for the decriminalization of abortion. As usual, Betty saw this choice slightly differently to other women: 'For me, the matter of choice has never been primarily the choice of abortion, but that you can choose to be a mother' (Friedan 2000).

Life as a single woman in wartime New York was wild, unpredictable and strangely exhilarating, but in 1945 when the war ended, Betty's position at Federated Press was given to a man returning home. A few months later, she landed a new position as reporter at the *UE News*, the weekly paper of the United Electrical, Radio and Machine Workers of America. She also landed a husband in Carl Friedan.

Then Comes Marriage

The marriage of Carl Friedan and Betty Goldstein was marked by passion, volatility, violence, alcohol and acrimony. Almost from the beginning, the two seemed an untenable match. Betty had been raised in Midwestern affluence and was an overspending, unapologetic intellectual; Carl had grown up in bitter Bostonian poverty and scraped through his adolescence practising magic in vaudeville shows. While Betty was landing scholarships at Smith and Berkeley, Carl attended University of Massachusetts and worked as a janitor at nearby Amherst College, before dropping out to attend Emerson College in Boston, majoring in theatre but never graduating.

In September 1942, he joined the US Army Signal Corps, hoping to avoid active combat but ended up in the 69th Regimental infantry, fighting in some of the bloodiest battles across Europe. He returned home in 1946 with a Bronze Star and began looking for work in the New York theatre world.

Be it divine providence or pot luck, Carl's only friend was Betty's co-worker at the Federated Press. The two met on a blind date. Betty fell hard for Carl and pursued him avidly. Carl wrote to his parents before they married that Betty wasn't much to look at, but she was bright enough so that he would never have to worry about money again. Even the wedding was a half-hearted affair; the couple married in a civil ceremony on 12 June 1947 in New York, then had a family wedding in Boston, organized by Carl's mother, whom Betty heartily disliked.

Despite the couple's near-constant fights and lack of money, their first child, Daniel, was born on 3 October 1948. Betty took an eight-month maternity leave from the *UE News* to throw herself into motherhood, but by summer 1949 she was back at work, her weekly $100 salary essential to the household. Carl had started a summer stock company where he managed and produced theatre shows, but he was never able to break into Broadway. Instead, he published an annual summer theatre handbook that morphed into a rather lacklustre career in advertising. Betty, on the other hand, loved her work at *UE News* writing stories on labour disputes, injustice in corporate America, and inequality in the workplace. She also covered the House Un-American Activities trial of the Hollywood Ten, a prominent list of directors and screenwriters who refused to answer questions about their communist affiliations and were subsequently banned and blacklisted from work in film. Since Betty had embraced Marxism in her college years and at Berkeley, she must have experienced great trepidation watching the trial and wondering what might happen to her in the great McCarthy witch hunt.

In 1951, the Friedans moved into Parkway Village in Queens, a development built to house United Nations employees and uniquely patterned on ideals of brotherhood, integration, and tolerance. Betty adored the community and, as she would throughout her life, she brought together a group of intellectual, carousing, and culturally fascinating friends who were committed to making life a madcap party. The six couples sent their children to the international school; talked, argued, protested, shared political ideas and artistic projects, and drank to excess. It was the closest thing to a commune Betty could imagine – a lifestyle filled with friends, food, booze, games and granular discussions of big issues. She would seek to recreate that same kind of community throughout her life and wherever she lived.

Unfortunately, Betty's wonderful community fell apart all too quickly. When she became pregnant again with son Jonathan in 1952, she lost her job at *UE News* and began a new career as a freelance writer for women's magazines. A few years later, the Friedans – now expecting their third child, Emily – moved out of their cramped but beloved Parkway apartment and into the exclusive country enclave of Rockland County, 35 miles north of Manhattan. Her revelatory experience of 1950s white, suburban stay- at-home housewives was about to begin.

Surburban Immersion

Betty was a genius at finding elaborate, intriguing and sometimes impractical places to live. Her first Rockland home was a beautiful old stone barn in Snedens Landing that hovered romantically over the Hudson River, but not so delightfully lacked any insulation. The family stayed for one frostbitten, budget-breaking winter, then bought an enormous four-bedroom, three-bathroom, gingerbread-trimmed house for $25,000 on an acre of land in Grandview-on-Hudson, an hour north of New York City.

Betty, who would almost always have a live-in maid (whom she refused to pay overtime), continued to write the tepid 'feminine' articles requested by the women's magazines, entertained grandly, and cultivated her relationship with the stimulating intellectual community in Rockland. In 1957, she founded the Community Resource Pool, an educational enrichment program years ahead of its time, which she originally founded to give her brilliant son Daniel more challenge than he was getting at school. The idea caught fire. Housed in the Rockland Center for the Arts, the CRP soon began attracting the best and brightest thinkers, leaders and artists in the country to lecture every Saturday on subjects as diverse as marine biology, Western civilization, outer space, art and sociology. Adults and children alike were galvanized by the intellectual ferment. The press was dazzled, and Betty, with her partner architectural historian James Fitch, was behind it all. Fitch said of Betty, 'She was brassy. She was always very dramatic. She had a big house on the edge of the river, and she had outrageous taste in décor – orange, red, purple – and dressed like that, too. Betty is an authentic home-grown radical' (Hennessee 1999).

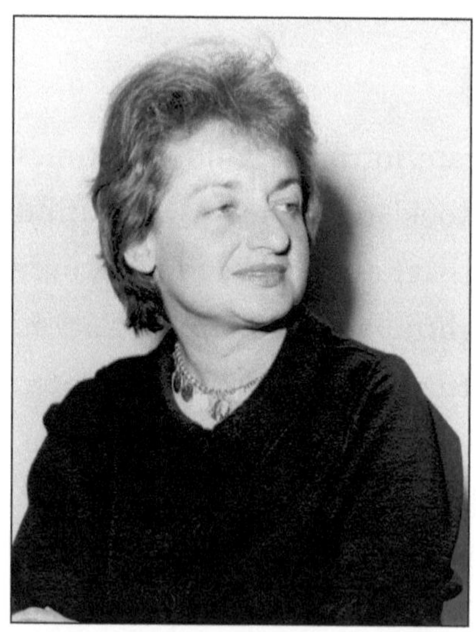

Fig. 1 Betty Friedan, 1960 (photographed by Fred Palumbo)

The CRP was Betty's first brush with fame. Her name was constantly in the papers, she made friends with some of the country's leading intellectuals, and she raised funds while she raised consciousness. At that heady moment, on fire with ideas, but insecure and thwarted in the limited way she was able to express them in her freelance magazine writing, Betty made the momentous decision to write something important. She decided to challenge the concept of 'The Togetherness Woman' (which served as the McCall's magazine tagline) and all that phrase promised, positing that women had given up too much of their identity in slavish service of others. As she struggled in the months afterwards to find a context and forum to express her insights, Betty found herself swimming directly against the conservative social mores of the time. Housework was being glorified as a woman's highest calling; breastfeeding was divinely ordained; and the American housewife was placed on a pedestal of femininity as confining as a girdle. This state of affairs would later be summed up by Betty as 'the feminine mystique'.

Realizing she had no chance of publishing her radical insights in women's magazines (that were expressly selling the concept of the happy housewife), Betty convinced George Brockway, president of W.W. Norton, to advance her $1,000 for a new book. 'She was the most ambitious woman I had ever met,' Brockway stated. 'She said that she didn't know what to call the subject exactly, but that it had something to do with a lack of identity, that women weren't being told... they aren't being allowed...' (Cohen 1988). Betty promised the book in a year, but with her exhaustive research, it ended up taking five. As usual, her timing was perfect.

The Feminine Mystique

Betty's groundbreaking book, *The Feminine Mystique*, was published in the USA on 19 February 1963, in a climate that was just beginning to explode with women's suppressed and repressed energy. The civil rights movement had begun in earnest. A young,

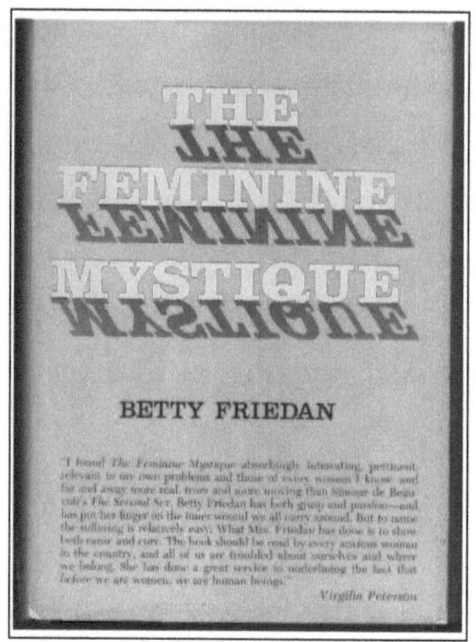

Fig. 2 *The Feminine Mystique*, published in 1963

liberal president had replaced an older wartime hero. Married women had just won access to contraceptives, and were questioning the strictures that insisted true femininity resided in passivity and subjugation. *The Feminine Mystique* didn't just hit a chord, it was a resounding gong heard around the world.

By the end of the year, 300,000 copies of the book had been sold and *The Feminine Mystique*'s author was a bona-fide celebrity. It should have been a triumphant time, but Betty's personal life was in tatters. Her women friends in Grandview-on-Hudson felt betrayed by the book's depiction of them as deluded drudges, particularly since many of them had volunteered to help her type and edit the book, while they also watched and fed the Friedan children. Her marriage, never on solid footing and marked by infidelity and tempestuous violence, was now truly falling apart. Both she and Carl were drinking heavily and often behaved badly under the influence. 'One night, when Carl was trying to throw me out of the car as we were driving home from some meeting, our friend Milton Carrow was driving by and made Carl stop,' she laconically remembered in *Life So Far*. In the same book she claims rarely to have made an appearance on TV during that time without a black eye, but later denied that she was a victim of domestic violence. In an interview with *The New York Times*, she said,

> *'He was no wife beater and I was no passive victim. We were both hot-tempered people... Unfortunately, he was bigger than me, so even if I started it, I ended up with the bruises. My daughter the doctor does not think I should make statements on domestic violence because I don't know the literature, but in my instance, it's all wrong to characterize our stormy marriage as any business of beating and victim. And I certainly am a stormy person.'* (Witchel 2000)

Now outcasts in Grandview, the Friedans moved back to New York City in 1964, into a lavish seven-room apartment in the renowned Dakota building (where John and Yoko Lennon would famously reside). Betty, with her usual real-estate radar, bought the apartment for just $15,000, and the couple threw themselves into the radical chic circle of beautiful people living there, entertaining in a spectacular style they certainly could not afford. The fighting and rancour continued unabated. 'I'm the bitch's husband,' Carl introduced himself to one guest. 'She's kind of doggy but she's very bright,' he confided to another (Hennessee 1999). With son Daniel at Princeton and the two younger children in the expensive private school of Dalton, the couple staggered through their new life in the limelight. Ironically, Betty seemed to be following precisely in the same overspending footsteps of her mother Miriam, with the concomitant ugly marital battles over money.

Life After the *Mystique*

Despite the overindulgent, overwrought and volatile state of the Friedan marriage, it would be seven more years until Betty screwed up the courage to finally divorce Carl. She persisted in her ambitious and demanding career, travelling around the country giving speeches and working nonstop to spearhead the women's movement. In June 1976, 12 years after a follow-up book to *The Feminine Mystique* was promised, Betty published *It Changed My Life*, a rather jumbled collection of essays, recollections and speeches she had given over the years. Her next book, *The Second Stage*, published in 1981, was prescient in many ways (predicting the need for shared parenting, work/life balance, and job flexitime) yet she still managed to flummox fellow feminists with her blithe assumption that the first stage, the liberation of women, was a fait accompli. In 1993, she published *The Fountain of Age*, a massive tome that represented years of research and grant-funded studies on creative aging. It stayed on *The New York Times* bestseller list for six weeks and was hailed as groundbreaking, but it failed to have a semblance of the impact of *The Feminine Mystique*. Her vivacious and unapologetic memoir, *Life So Far*, was published in 2000, six years before her death.

Regardless of the lacklustre reception of her later books, Betty's fulsome intellectual curiosity and charisma were the hallmarks of her life. She never stopped inspiring passionate conversations, think tanks, conferences and seminars about architecture, aging, psychology, labour unions, income inequality, pornography, the media, and of course, women. She travelled the world and continued to teach, talk and lead. 'For the rest of her life she would continue to search for concepts that applied feminism to the larger society…to keep the dialogue going.' (Hennessee 1999) In her personal life, she found financial stability and family reconciliation at last, spending summers in her rustic home in

Sag Harbor, New York with her three married children, eight beloved grandchildren, and sometimes even Carl.

Even after their divorce, her ex-husband was in awe of her accomplishments, if also clear-headed about her personality. As Carl Friedan explains,

> *'She changed the course of history almost singlehandedly. It took a driven, super aggressive, egocentric, almost lunatic dynamo to rock the world the way she did. Unfortunately, she was that same person at home, where that kind of conduct doesn't work. She simply never understood this.'* (Ginsberg 2000)

Speaking of her own difficulties in relationships with men, Betty acknowledged a different reason: '...having been married to somebody who was pretty threatened when I began to get famous, I'm leery of subjecting someone to that' (Witchel 2000).

After her divorce Betty did have a series of relationships with men, some married and some not, but she never remarried. She also attempted to make peace with other feminists she had previously alienated, specifically Gloria Steinem, Kate Millett and Bella Abzug. Some hatchets were buried; others, not so much.

In 2000, reflecting on the realities of her life in comparison to young women of the 21st century, she said,

> *'Young women today take for granted opportunities that my generation never dreamed of. I hear them say, "I'm not a feminist, but I'm going to law school"... "I'm not a feminist but I'll get married when I choose, if I choose."... She's not a feminist, but choice, autonomy, ambition and*

> *opportunity are her subtext.'* (Friedan, quoted in *The Indianapolis Star,* 11 June 2000)

Despite their blithe refutation of feminism, this was precisely the change for women Friedan had worked to achieve.

Betty Friedan died on 4 February 2006, surrounded by her three children. The cause of death was heart failure, though it seems impossible to believe that Betty's heart ever failed her.

Betty Friedan's Timeline

Betty Friedan

- **1921** Bettye Goldstein is born in Peoria, Illinois
- **1938** Graduates from High School
- **1942** Graduates from Smith College and heads to UC Berkeley
- **1943** Moves to New York and begins working at Federated Press as a labour journalist
- **1946** Loses job to returning veteran; goes to work for UE News
- **1947** Marries Carl Friedan
- **1948** First son, Daniel, is born
- **1952** Fired from UE News when she becomes pregnant with Jonathan
- **1953** Begins work as a freelance journalist with women's magazines
- **1956** Family moves to Rockland County suburbs; daughter, Emily, is born
- **1957** Distributes lengthy questionnaire at 15th reunion of Smith College
- **1958** Signs contract with Norton Publishing to write a book on women's desperation

World Events

- **1920** Women get the vote in America
- **1929** The Great Depression begins
- **1939** World War II breaks out
- **1945** World War II ends
- **1947** McCarthy era begins, investigating suspected Communists
- **1949** Simone de Beauvoir publishes ***The Second Sex***
- **1950** Korean War begins; baby boom in US
- **1954** Trials for birth-control pill begin
- **1960** Birth control pill approved by FDA

1963 Publishes ***The Feminine Mystique***

1966 Co-founds NOW and is named president

1969 Co-founds NARAL; divorces Carl

1970 Loses presidency of NOW; organizes Women's March in NYC

1971 Co-founds NWPC

1976 Publishes ***It Changed My Life***

1981 Publishes ***The Second Stage***

1993 Publishes ***The Fountain of Age***

1997 Co-publishes ***Beyond Gender***

2000 Publishes ***Life So Far***

2006 Betty Friedan dies on her 85th birthday

1964 Civil Rights Act passes, prohibiting job discrimination on the basis of sex

1971 Gloria Steinem founds *Ms*. magazine

1972 Congress passes Equal Rights Amendment, but 38 states must ratify

1973 Roe vs. Wade legalizes women's right to abortion

1976 *TIME* magazine gives it's 'Man of the Year' nomination to American women

1977 First National Women's Conference held

1980 Ronald Reagan elected President

1982 Equal Rights Amendment fails

1991 Gulf War begins

2001 September 11 terrorist attacks

2. Influences on Friedan's Thinking

Like many influential thinkers whose ideas have changed history, Friedan often insisted on the singular originality of her feminist concepts and of the women's movement itself, distinct from all previous revolutions and social movements.

> *'There are no blueprints for our revolution, not from Karl Marx or any of the other ideologues of exploited classes, for the relationship of woman to man is not the same as that of worker to boss, of oppressed to oppressor, of black to white. We can only find our blueprint from our own unique experience.'* (Friedan 1976)

However, a wide swath of writers, philosophers, psychologists and first feminists had a profound influence on Friedan's thinking, and one of her great strengths was her deep thirst for new ideas and her willingness to embrace them.

From her earliest years, Betty was a prolific reader, gobbling up *Little Women*, *The Railway Children*, and endless titles in series such as *The Bobbsey Twins* and *Nancy Drew*. In high school and college, she took numerous writing, poetry and literature courses, reading American novelists such as John Steinbeck, John Roderigo Dos Passos and Thomas Wolfe, but she found her true calling in psychology.

The New Psychology: Koffka, Lewin & Erikson

The decade of the 1940s was a dynamic developmental period in modern psychology, as scores of hugely influential psychologists, philosophers, scientists and historians fled from Germany, Austria, and France to escape facism and were welcomed by American universities. New theories of group behaviour (studying conformity, conflict, compromise and cohesion); of attitudes and beliefs (how they are formed, coalesce, alter and change); and of social and self-perception (introducing humanistic and cultural considerations to therapy) were formulated by psychologists like Erich Fromm, B.F. Skinner, Abraham Maslow, Carl Rogers and Alfred Kinsey. In her undergraduate and graduate college years, Betty was privileged to study under three giants of modern psychological theory: Kurt Koffka (1886–1941), Kurt Lewin (1890–1947), and Erik Erikson (1902–1994).

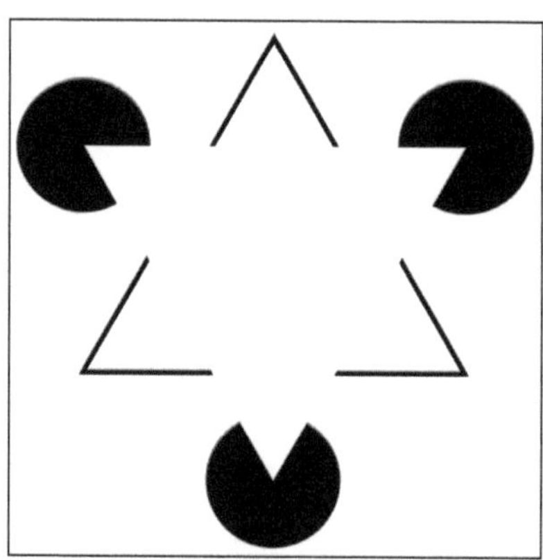

Fig. 3 The Kanizsa Triangle is famously used to illustrate how the mind 'sees' objects that are not there, because of its tendency to complete the gestalt, or whole. Scientists believe that this is because the brain is trained to scan the environment for potential threat, and 'fill in' a break in lines to 'see' a whole object.

Kurt Koffka, born and raised in Berlin, was one of the principal architects of Gestalt psychology and emigrated to America in 1924 to teach at Cornell University. He penned the now-famous quote, 'The whole is other than the sum of its parts' and helped define a new way of understanding, perception and human experience that insisted on taking into account the totality of the ego, cultural context and the behavioural environment.

Friedan would later apply this theory to Freud, arguing that he was unable to see the cultural context and behavioural environment in which he himself lived, so he did not realize that his opinions were influenced by the zeitgeist, and that his patients were living within and responding to the same zeitgeist. Koffka was Betty's professor at Smith in her junior year, and his thinking was a huge influence on her own. When Koffka died in her senior year, it was Betty who wrote 'the editorial eulogy that emphasized the challenge and excitement of his course' (Horowitz 2000). Many years later, Betty wrote,

> *'Kurt Koffka and the elegant conceptual structure of Gestalt psychology made me feel like some kind of mental mountain goat, leaping from peak to peak... I learned, forever, that the whole is more than the sum of its parts, that human behavior can only be understood in its cultural context, that our vision cannot be wholly objective.'* (Friedan 2000)

There is always more than one way to see something: the perspective with which we approach something altering what we see. This idea is often explained by the illustration of the Rubin Vase, as shown in Fig. 4.

The summer following her class with Koffka, Betty spent in Iowa City working with Kurt Lewin, a pioneer in organizational development and 'group dynamics' (he coined that phrase, arguing that a group was more than just a collection of individuals and had its own specific characteristics). Lewin is also regarded as the founder of social psychology, which explores the human mind within the context of other humans and societies. Lewin's famous equation, B

Fig. 4 The Rubin Vase can be seen in two ways, revealing either the silhouette of a vase in black or the profiles of faces in white.

$= f(P, E)$, states that behaviour is a function of the person in his or her environment, eschewing any idea that a person's behaviour is determined by the individual alone. Betty's work with Lewin in Iowa was with children, exploring how groups are established, governed, interact and develop. 'Very early,' Betty says, 'I saw proof of the inferiority of autocratic, authoritarian leadership as opposed to a participatory democratic model, not as a matter of ideological litany but tested in problem-solving experiments' (Friedan 2000). Lewin's experiments in changing behaviour were the foundation for the emerging field of 'sensitivity training' that would be used to combat religious and racial prejudice. He had a profound understanding of social problems and pioneered the concept of action research to move constructively from problem to solution – a premise Betty adopted with gusto.

Another powerful influence was Erik Erikson, the brilliant child psychoanalyst. Betty studied with him while in graduate school at Berkeley, during the time he was exploring society, culture and the development of identity. Another German-born Jew, Erikson only learned in late childhood that the Jewish man he considered his father was actually not his biological parent, and that his mother had conceived him out of wedlock with a non-Jewish Dane. Not surprisingly, Erikson became obsessed with the concept of identity in child development and did groundbreaking work with

Native-American children, connecting the fields of psychology and anthropology. Erikson coined the phrase 'identity crisis' to describe a failure in healthy ego development during adolescence and spent his career studying how people learn, grow, adjust and hopefully progress through eight psychosocial (as opposed to Freud's psychosexual) life-stages.

All three psychologists – Koffka, Lewin and Erikson – would influence Betty's later endeavours, as her books and activism explored the totality (Gestalt) of women's place in American culture. She looked at women within society, rather than simply on an individual basis, and charted their historical struggle for identity. Taking Lewin's words on the need to actively construct solutions to any identified problems, she then helped to create, organize and lead women's movements around the world (in a brilliant illustration of group dynamics).

In her own words, Friedan 'learned from Kurt Koffka at Smith, and then Kurt Lewin in Iowa, and Erik Erikson at Berkeley how to look at any phenomenon... in its total, concrete, cultural context: the gestalt' (Friedan 1976).

College Revelations

Betty's choice of Smith, an elite women's college, also meant she was in a place where every position of power, every club leadership, and every top honour was earned by a woman. That experience of women's proficiency was profound, and the expectation of female excellence was intrinsic to the place. 'At Smith...I was taken seriously as a person and inculcated with an ineradicable sense of responsibility for the human destiny, and my own power to affect it' (Friedan 1976).

One of Betty's other Smith professors, Dr. Dorothy Wolff Douglas, taught an Economics course called 'Theories and Movements for Social Reconstruction' which suggested that social welfare programs and strong labour unions were the most viable way to combat the spread of fascism, which had just taken hold in Italy and Germany. Betty was deeply influenced by her radically left-wing Jewish professor, who also was the mother of four children, an author, a partner in an equitable and competitive marriage, and an ardent proponent of two brand new ideas in Betty's world: equal pay for equal work for women, and economic compensation for household work.

At Dr. Douglas's urging, in the summer of her sophomore year, Betty spent eight weeks at the Highlander Folk School in Monteagle, Tennessee, a centre for teaching social justice that in the 1940s was focused on labour movements and labour organizing. This school would later train some of the most important figures in the civil rights movements of the USA, including Dr. Martin Luther King, Jr., John Lewis, and Rosa Parks. The school's setting in poor, rural Appalachia was an eye-opening experience in itself for Betty, and its heady mix of workers, grassroots leaders, community organizers, educators and researchers all discussing injustice, war, inequality and class struggle was intoxicating to Betty. She took her new awareness back to Smith and continued to write, with a decidedly Marxist bent, on labour issues and unionization for the next 10 years, first on the college paper, and then in New York City.

> *'I remember that sharp distinction I had learned in my economics class at Smith where I studied communism, fascism, capitalism – that fascism was capitalism carried*

> *to the extreme, absolute power to those who owned the industries and banks, no freedom of the people to organize or express dissent ... we learned that communism was a system that put the interests of the people first and in which private profit from the exploitation of workers was abolished.'* (Friedan 2000)

Radical Politics

Betty's fascination with Marxism and subsequent deep dive into radical labour and union politics would last until the early 1950s. Yet despite her description of herself as growing up 'very political, very involved, consciously radical' (Horowitz 2000), Betty was also '...that girl with all A's and I wanted boys worse than anything' (Horowitz 2000). So perhaps it is not surprising that in the one year (1942) that Betty spent in a graduate program in Berkeley, her most important influence, besides Erik Erikson, was undoubtedly the boyfriend who persuaded her to give up a coveted scholarship that would have funded her through her PhD in psychology. He coyly threatened, 'You can take that fellowship but you know I'll never get one like it. You know what it will do to us' (Hennessee 1999). Putting herself second for the greater good of 'us', Betty promptly quit graduate school. Before long the erstwhile romance evaporated, and she returned home to Peoria, briefly suffering a revisitation of the humiliation of her early high-school days.

In late 1943, Betty moved to New York, where she landed a job as assistant news editor for the Federated Press, digging up stories for labour, liberal and radical newspapers across America. 'As a Popular Front labour journalist ... she saw the trade union movement as the vanguard of progressive social activism' (Horowitz 2000). She covered General Electric's 'price-fixing', General Motors' efforts to eviscerate labour's power, and industry attempts across America to provoke strikes in order to break the unions. After the emotional devastation she had felt in leaving Berkeley and dropping out of her PhD program, the writing and reporting work made her feel alive again, even if she derided the lack of status in her position. 'The labor newspaper jobs I didn't consider 'career' at all. They were just something I could do, liked doing' (Friedan 2000). She also covered women's issues, focusing on black, Latina and white working-class women and the challenges they faced in unionizing and earning equal pay, as well as penning a helpful and lively 'Wartime Living' column that counselled women on what was on sale, and how to stretch a dollar to cover the family budget.

Many of Betty's wartime articles sound as if they could have been written today. Horowitz notes that she

> *'envisioned progressive forces working together ... She hailed the effort of organized labour, the NAACP, the National Lawyers' Guild, the League of Women's Shoppers, and the Women's Trade Union League to fight for progressive taxation. She revealed the discrimination against Mexican Americans and Japanese Americans. She reported on the deplorable conditions under which migrant workers lived... she honored the efforts of African American children and their parents ... to fight against segregated and patently unequal education.'* (Horowitz 2000)

Despite her aptitude for journalism, in 1946, with men coming home from war to reclaim the jobs they'd left, Betty lost her job with Federated Press. The onset of McCarthyism was also leading Federated Press to 'let go' its more radical, outspoken writers, so Betty's clearly Marxist leanings may also have played a part in her demise. However, she soon secured another job as a reporter for the United Electrical, Radio and Machine Workers of America's paper, the weekly *UE News*.

The UE was a radical union at a critical moment; an avowedly Communist-led organization, it had just fomented post-war strikes to shut down all Westinghouse and General Electric factories in the USA and Canada. The backlash was swift and ferocious. 'Beginning in 1946, Friedan witnessed the efforts by federal agencies, congressional committees, major corporations, the Roman Catholic Church and the CIO to break the radical leadership of the UE' (Horowitz 2000). While labour regarded the power of unions as essential to promoting progressive social change that would benefit the working class, minorities and women, business saw the labour movement as an existential threat to profits, as well as an anti-capitalist Communist plot.

Betty threw herself into the fray. She celebrated the 1946 formation of The Congress of American Women, a cross-class and racially integrated organization of progressives. She wrote real-life stories on wage discrimination, exposed racism and religious discrimination on the job and in society, and authored a 39-page pamphlet decrying the exploitation of women workers by corporations, titled 'UE Fights for Women Workers'. In this she detailed the appalling conditions of Latina and African-American factory workers, and a year later, her shorter pamphlet, 'Women Fight for a Better Life!' addressed the childcare problems that all working female parents faced. 'In the world of progressive and labour feminism familiar to Friedan in the late 1940s and early 1950s...women's issues were widely debated, providing key concepts, language and tools of analysis that would shape what she wrote in *The Feminine Mystique* (Horowitz 2000).

From War to Wary America

The transformative years of WWII and the post-war environment of America had a profound effect on the gestalt of Betty Friedan's experience. During the war, the sense of purpose, community, and shared sacrifice brought Americans together. Approximately 37 per cent of all women were working, and despite wartime fear and anxiety, people were fully engaged. Political perceptions were also changing. The long, hard years of the Depression had shaken many Americans' faith in capitalism. Progressives feared authoritarianism and fascism, freely expressed in the Axis powers, far more than communism and socialism, and there was a fluidity of experimentation with all manner of political systems and theories. But that all came to a screeching halt in the late 1940s.

'"Security" was a big part of what began to happen in 1949,' Betty would later write, '...as in atomic secrets, Communist espionage, the House Un-American Activities Committee, loyalty oaths, and the beginning of blacklists for writers' (Friedan 1976).

She explains further:

> *'McCarthyism, the danger of war against Russia and of fascism in America, and the reality of US imperial, corporate wealth and power all made men and women who used to have large visions of making the whole world over uncomfortable with the Old Left rhetoric of revolution.'* (Friedan 1976)

Progressives, radicals and sympathizers all came under attack.

> *'For those who were not subject to its power, it is difficult to imagine the force and recklessness of McCarthyism in the late 1940s and 1950s. It ruined the lives of Communists, ex-Communists, suspected Communists, fellow travelers and Popular Front participants. People committed suicide...writers were denied the ability to learn a living...Investigators, authorized and unauthorized, haunted and pursued people they suspected of subversive or disloyal behavior.'* (Horowitz 2000)

In response, Americans went underground, both psychologically and politically. After the horrors of the war and the bomb, Americans gratefully hunkered down in their new surburban homes and focused on security, conformity, their children, and the perfection of their backyards and barbecues. 'Amid this surfeit of family values, the economy produced wondrous new devices, streams of cars and appliances and gadgets for the deprived children of the Depression who might never have had such things and wanted them—and thus became hostages to them.' (Hennessee 1999) As Friedan summarizes: 'Suburbia, exurbia, with the children as an excuse—there was a comfortable small world you could really do something about.' (Friedan 1976) Women were exhorted to return to lives of traditional domesticity and dedicate themselves to their husbands and children.

Outside Voices

However, distinctly feminist voices were also rising. In 1949, Simone de Beauvoir's groundbreaking *The Second Sex* was published in France and quickly translated into English for sale across Europe and America. Beauvoir, a revered French intellectual and existentialist, wrote her epic, sprawling treatise to examine how women have been defined throughout history – in literature, mythology, science and by design – only by their relationship to men, the first and primary sex. 'The fundamental source of women's oppression is its historical and social construction as the quintessential Other,' Beauvoir reasoned. She argued that through the ages, men have consciously and purposefully stereotyped women as dependent and unknowable in order to establish power over them. This was framed and enforced through the laws, customs and social norms of a patriarchy, and by the application of a false aura of 'mystery' to women – an idea that would be equally captivating to Friedan in understanding post-war American women.

> *'When I first read* The Second Sex *in the early fifties...the book's effect on me was so depressing that I felt like going back to bed...and pulling the covers up over my head. Only after a dozen years...did I personally, concretely, analyze what had brought me and other American women to that depressing state. And then I saw it as something that could be changed.'* (Friedan 1976)

Beauvoir's book was sweeping, relentless, original and radical. She eschewed motherhood, unequivocally stating, 'In my opinion, as long as the family and the myth of the family and...motherhood and the maternal instinct are not destroyed, women will still be oppressed' (Beauvoir in Friedan 1976). She calmly proposed that the only way to change the traditional system was 'to fight and destroy it'.

Betty Friedan perhaps took a similarly grim view of women's retreat into motherhood and the home, yet she shared none of the same radical ideology with Beauvoir. In fact, Friedan's entire life's work after the publication of *The Feminine Mystique* as an organizer, activist and feminist was focused on making the women's movement as mainstream as possible, pivoting sharply away from the radical left, Marxism and authoritarianism. Betty never wanted to alienate men or bring the system down – she adored men and sex, loved being a mother, and revered the idea of family, even while challenging the orthodoxy that insisted women's identity be confined to those arenas.

From Labour to Women's Liberation

What prompted Betty's evolution from radical labour journalist to prophet of women's self-actualization? In 1952, she was fired from *UE News* for being pregnant, and with a depressing recurrence of her asthma, she undertook intense psychotherapy that led her to focus on a more authentic and personal path to identity. Betty was also, like multitudes of fellow activists, undoubtedly influenced by the political events of the time that were both disillusioning and terrifying to anyone who could be targeted as a communist or radical. In a short space of time she had three young children to worry about, which as any mother can attest, can diminish one's ability to pursue anything more theoretical than toilet training. 'I began to feel an aversion to any and all political dogma that didn't seem to come from real life.' (Friedan 2000)

Following a gut-instinct epiphany brought on by reading the questionnaires she had given to her fellow Smith alumnae in 1957, Betty went to the New York Public Library and started her book.

The more she wrote, the more she needed to research; and the more she read, the more she accessed, absorbed and analyzed the ideas of people who had most influenced contemporary thinking about women. It would become a five-year journey. However, after she sent her first draft to Burton Beals, her editor at Norton, he encouraged her to add a chapter on her closest predecessors: that amazing chorus line of suffragettes and original feminists who, from the 1800s through the early 1900s, worked tirelessly for women's rights and the vote. That discovery rocked her world.

The Fire of the First Feminists

Betty was overwhelmed by what she didn't know about the lives of the first foremothers, and then enraged that it had been kept an open secret.

> *'It says something about the power of the feminine mystique, already blotting out the historical reality of women... that this particular summa cum laude graduate of Smith had never studied the documents, records, biographies of any of those feminist foremothers in all my years at that best-of-all American women's colleges.' (*Friedan 2000)

Betty was staggered by the women's courage and zeal, as well as by the almost unimaginable odds they had faced.

> *'They had to prove that women were human ...not a passive, empty mirror...not a mindless animal, not a thing...incapable of a voice in her own existence, before they could even begin to fight for the rights women needed to become the human equals of men.'* (Friedan 1963)

Challenging 'the perversion of history that the passion and fire of the feminist movement came from man-hating, embittered, sex-starved spinsters' (Friedan 1963) – a perception that would soon be hurled at Second-Wave feminists as well – she set out to understand the women who had walked this path before her. She promised, 'it is this first journey which holds the clue to much that has happened to women since...to recognize the reality of the passion that moved those women to leave home in search of new identity, or, staying home, to yearn bitterly for something more' (Friedan 1963). Friedan could hear the 'reality of that passion' in those first feminists as clearly as she noticed its utter absence in the suburban housewives that she was interviewing.

Betty was deeply moved by the suffragettes' individual stories of commitment and courage, and also by the genesis of the movement, rooted as it was in anti-slavery crusades and women's education. She noted that, 'it is an undeniable fact that, in organizing, petitioning and speaking out to free the slaves, American women learned how to free themselves' (Friedan 1963). She loved the story of Lucretia Mott (mother of five) and Elizabeth Stanton (on her honeymoon) who upon being relegated to seats behind a curtain at a men-only, anti-slavery convention in London 'decided that it was not only the slaves who needed to be liberated' (Friedan 1963). The two ladies went on to launch the women's rights movement in 1848 at the groundbreaking Seneca Falls Convention.

That experience surely resonated in Betty's brain when the African-American civil rights movement began to coalesce around the nation in the 1950s. She studied the actions of the women who had first dared to speak out in public, such as

Ernestine Rose, the Jewish daughter of a Polish rabbi who fled to England to be free and educate herself (then supported herself, her husband, and her anti-slavery and women's equality causes with a thriving aromatherapy business). And demure and dainty Lucy Stone, who taught school for $1 a week for eight years until she could finally afford college and became the first woman in Massachusetts to graduate (from Oberlin) before becoming a lauded anti-slavery proponent, speaker, lobbyist and organizer. And the aforementioned Elizabeth Cady Stanton, now a jolly and devoted mother of six, who dared voice her discontent with women's truncated opportunities trapped in the home, and whose honest writing activated hundreds of 'housewives and daughters who...came in wagons from a radius of fifty miles to hear her speak' (Friedan 1963).

Betty also took heed of the tactics used to silence and shame those women activists: the dogmatic insistence from church and clergy that women were Biblically-called to be subservient to men; the denigrating contention that women's rights were only sought by pathetic women who couldn't attract a husband; and the fear-mongering predictions that liberated women would destroy society and the family. She certainly studied Eleanor Flexner's *Century of Struggle*, published in 1959, which was a comprehensive and deeply detailed history of the roots of feminism and feminists from the colonial times until the 1920s. In her study of the First Wave of feminism, Friedan would be both inspired and forewarned of what was to come in the Second Wave.

Friedan also learned something about tenacity and persistence from that First Wave that she would take into her 50 years of struggle, setbacks, searing defeats, and soaring triumphs. In the American suffragettes' 70-year battle to get the vote, those women had

> *'conducted five campaigns of referenda to male voters; 480 campaigns to get legislatures to submit suffrage amendments to voters; 277 campaigns to get state party conventions to include woman's suffrage planks; 30 campaigns to get presidential party conventions to adopt woman's suffrage planks; and 19 campaigns with 19 successive Congresses.'* (Flexner 1996)

The final two people who helped shape Friedan's thinking about women were so influential she devoted a chapter to each in *The Feminine Mystique*. Anthropologist Margaret Mead (1901–1978) and psychoanalyst Sigmund Freud (1856–1939) both had a monumental impact on American society and were ubiquitous in the culture, but that did not prevent Betty from taking a hammer to their theories when she felt it was justified. 'I wonder now that I had the nerve to take on Margaret Mead...' she later admitted (Friedan 2000).

Mining Margaret Mead

Betty cited Margaret Mead as 'the most powerful influence on modern women...felt in almost every layer of American thought' (Friedan 1963). Originally, Margaret Mead's early writing and anthropological studies seriously challenged gender orthodoxy, thrilling Friedan with 'the realization of the enormous plasticity of the human condition, male and female, our amazingly large, various and, in the end, similar human potential' (Friedan 2000).

In her many studies of Samoan and other indigenous cultures, Mead uncovered convincing evidence that sexual mores are a cultural construct, women's sexuality and reproduction are natural and healthy, and women are not seen in all societies as passive and subservient. These findings bolstered the intellectual underpinnings of the sexual revolution and feminism, and inspired the liberating movements that promoted natural childbirth, breastfeeding and birth-control. But Friedan bemoaned what she saw as the big turnaround in Mead's consciousness after her exposure to Freudian thought and analysis. After that experience, Mead began to vociferate 'the suddenly ineradicable boundaries of female fulfillment through a woman's biological capacity to have a child and her warning of a dire fate to society when an individual defies or denies that ordained female destiny' (Friedan 2000).

> *'I saw how they took the craze for motherhood and suburbia and repudiation of career in those 15 years after World War II and converted it into a "functional" absolute: man the breadwinner, woman the housewife, man the doer, woman the be-er.'* (Friedan 2000)

Margaret Mead was everywhere in 1950s America – in newspaper articles, books, scholarly journals and glossy women's magazines – and paradoxically, over time, her proclamations often contradicted each other. Should women stay content in the home, there to bandage tiny knees and man-sized egos, or should she be out in the world, taking on critical issues such as nuclear disarmament to protect her own children, and those of the enemy? Mead advocated both scenarios with conviction, yet her words provided the scientific authority for limiting women's potential and keeping their role domestic, distinct and uncompetitive with men.

That stranglehold of subservient domesticity, for Friedan, was the bridge that led directly to 'the mystique'.

3. The Problem That Has No Name

In 1960s America, editors, educators and physicians began to grapple with the fact that thousands of well-off women were acutely depressed but unable to say why this was so. Friedan was to reach her own conclusion:

> '...*the problem that has no name stirring in the minds of so many American women today is not a matter of loss of femininity or too much education, or the demands of domesticity...It is the key to these other new and old problems which have been torturing women and their husbands and children, and puzzling their doctors and educators for years. It may well be the key to our future as a nation and a culture. We can no longer ignore that voice within women that says, 'I want something more than my husband and my children and my home.'* (Friedan 1963)

The publication of Betty's Friedan's book, *The Feminine Mystique*, in February 1963, was a blockbuster event. Almost overnight, this woman with the rapier wit, rapid-fire delivery, and disturbing views on the psychic state of American women seemed to be everywhere – on television, radio, lecture circuits and book signings, from sea to shining sea. Friedan's wild literary success was particularly notable because *The Feminine Mystique* was not a titillating potboiler or Hollywood confessional; it was a scholarly, dense and challenging polemical tome. Yet the book obviously connected with women on an almost visceral level, even while it painted a painfully yearning portrait of affluent white American women.

Friedan was hardly the first writer to grasp that something was fundamentally amiss with contemporary American society that appeared so placid on the surface. Critical books on the negative influence of conformity and capitalism in the 1950s included *The Man in the Grey Flannel Suit*, *The View from the 40th Floor*, *The Hidden Persuaders* and *The Organization Man*. But those books, as Friedan was only too aware, concentrated on men. The idea of 'women's issues' was only just beginning to bubble to the surface, in spite of the relentless messaging in women's magazines, television, and books extolling the virtues and satisfaction of the happy American housewife. Why would these women have issues? The consensus view was that they had everything!

In the Grip of the Mystique

In 1952, as Betty attempted to straddle early motherhood with working for a living, she took on freelance writing opportunities for a proliferation of women's magazines (and their male editors). Here, her real education in the miasma of the mystique began.

Women's magazines in the 1950s were a bright and shiny homage to American consumerism and to the contented housewives behind all those beautiful appliances and household goods. *Redbook*, *McCall's*, *Ladies' Home Journal* and *Good*

Housekeeping celebrated the mass retreat of women into the home, marriage and motherhood with stories like 'Have Babies While You're Young,' 'How to Snare a Male,' and 'Femininity Begins at Home.' Educators, communities, and the media alike promoted 'pretty pictures of the American housewife, kissing their husbands goodbye in front of the picture window, depositing their station wagons full of children at school, and smiling as they ran the new electric waxer across the spotless kitchen floor' (Friedan, 1963). Readers quickly learned 'that truly feminine women do not want careers, higher education, political rights – the independence and the opportunities that the old-fashioned feminists fought for' (Friedan, 1963).

Women who did choose careers instead of motherhood were ignored in those magazines, or profiled as suffering terrible emotional consequences for that selfish decision (usually losing their husbands to a frilly-aproned, cookie-baking gal). As Friedan noted, this represented a profound shift away from the editorial content of a mere decade earlier, when women's magazines had featured hundreds of articles on topics as far-ranging and worldly as American diplomacy, Russian aggression, the invasion of Czechoslovakia, the New Deal, poet Carl Sandburg and the battle for birth control. What had happened to replace intelligent content with saccharine portraits of passive female contentment?

> *'I found a clue one morning, sitting in the office of a women's magazine editor – a woman who, older than I, remembers the days when the old image was being created, and who had watched it being displaced. The old image of the spirited career girl was largely created*

> *by writers and editors who were women, she told me. The new image of woman as housewife-mother has been largely created by writers and editors who are men.'* (Friedan, 1963)

The 1940s ideal of a liberated woman, empowered by suffrage and an entry into the working world, was rejected with literary vigour. *Look* magazine's issue of 16 October 1956 gushed over the new American woman's docility:

> *'No longer a psychological immigrant to man's world, she works, rather casually, as a third of the US labor force, less towards a "big career" than as a way of filling a hope chest or buying a new home freezer. She gracefully concedes the top jobs to men. This wondrous creature also marries younger than ever, bears more babies and looks and acts far more feminine than the 'emancipated' girl of the 1920s or even 30s.'* (Friedan, 1963)

This repeatedly parroted and drastically truncated vision of femininity got through to its audience. 'In the 15 years after World War II, the mystique of feminine fulfillment became the cherished and self-perpetuating core of contemporary American culture' Friedan noted (1963). During this time, the average age at which American women married dipped to 20. Between 1920 and 1958, the proportion of women going to college decreased by almost 25 per cent, and by the mid-50s, 60 per cent of female college students were dropping out before graduation. Instead of two or three children, women were now having four or five. Between 1940 and 1947, the reproductive rate of women college graduates increased 81 per cent. By 1960, America's birthrate was overtaking India's. These trends were heartily embraced.

> *'The suburban housewife – she was the dream image of young American women and the envy, it was said, of women all over the world...She was healthy, beautiful, educated, concerned only about her husband, her children, her home. She had found true feminine fulfillment.'* (Friedan 1963)

Yet beneath the surface, there was trouble in American paradise, manifested in the inexplicable misery of those same middle-class and wealthy women living lives of seeming endless affluence.

Lives of Quiet Desperation

In the same year as *Look*'s poetic paean, the editors of *McCall's* ran a short article called 'The Mother Who Ran Away,' and the article attracted the highest readership of any article *McCall's* had ever run. 'We suddenly realized that all those women at home with their three and a half children were miserably unhappy,' said a former editor (Friedan, 1963).

By 1960, 'the problem that has no name burst like a boil through the image of the happy American housewife' (Friedan, 1963). *Redbook* magazine, as a promotional stunt, invited its readers to answer the question 'Why Young Mothers Feel Trapped' in order to win $500. The editors were stunned to receive 24,000 entries from women writing eloquently about their longing to break free of their homes. Before long, the media were not questioning what delicious recipes American housewives were whipping up for dinner, but whence came the despair and sadness of these mysterious females. 'What the heck is wrong with women today?' 'What more could they possibly want?'

Friedan was certain the right questions were not being asked.

> *'I do not accept the answer that there is no problem because American women have luxuries that women in other times and lands never dreamed of; part of the strange newness of the problem is that it cannot be understood in terms of the age-old material problems of man: poverty, sickness, hunger, cold. The women who suffer this problem have a hunger that food cannot fill.'* (Friedan, 1963)

She decided to take a deeper look into the problem, fuelled by her own intuition and the sense that she was destined for this work. 'A Geiger counter clicked in my own inner ear when I could not fit the quiet desperation of so many women into the picture of the modern American housewife that I myself was helping to create, writing for the women's magazines.' (Friedan 1963) In hundreds of conversations with women of all ages, incomes, and backgrounds she began to probe what had happened to shift women away from the empowered path they had taken in the 1940s and back into the passive position of the Victorian age. Where others found the elusive quality of the problem impossible to pin down, Friedan was able to put a name and face on it. In doing so, she also revealed some uncomfortable and illuminating truths about the lives of white, wealthy, suburban women in America, mainly because she took the time to listen to them with seriousness and compassion. The women she spoke to all assumed that there must be something wrong with them, or their marriage (which would also be their fault). Because, after all, they had everything! Friedan heard their bewilderment and their desperation as she recorded their words:

> *'I seem to sleep so much. I don't know why I should be so tired. This house isn't nearly so hard to clean as the cold-water flat we had when I was working...'*
>
> *'I just don't feel alive.'*
>
> *'...there's nothing to look forward to.'*
>
> *'I'm so ashamed.'*
>
> *'I must be hopelessly neurotic.'*
>
> *'...I'm desperate. I begin to feel like I have no personality. I'm a server of food and a putter-on of pants and a bedmaker, somebody who can be called on when you want something. But who am I?'*
>
> *'I ask myself why I'm so dissatisfied.'*
>
> *'I feel empty somehow...incomplete.'*
>
> *'I feel like crying without any reason.'*
>
> *'I feel as if I don't exist.'*

Clearly, women's pain and confusion was visceral and authentic. However, their sense of shame and guilt about feeling intensely depressed, despite living a seemingly perfect life, stopped them from talking openly about it. Every woman thought it was just her lonely and pathetic problem. Societally, the blame was put squarely on the woman who couldn't adjust.

How had it all happened? How had these women ended up back in the home, meekly accepting the decree that every woman's feminine calling was to be a wife and mother, and nothing more? Was there something about this particular idea of femininity that was causing such anguish in its loyal followers? But how could this be so, when Freud had memorably stated that for women, 'anatomy is destiny' and even St. Peter in the Bible said 'likewise, ye wives, be in subjection to your own husbands'? Wasn't female submission bred in the bone, a woman's biological and psychological destiny?

It took someone with the insight, psychological prowess, dogged determination and chutzpah of Betty Friedan to challenge the myth of femininity being peddled and to identify, explore, explode, reframe and offer a solution to 'the problem with no name'.

Solving the Invisible Problem

Of course, Friedan wasn't alone in investigating the mystery of women's deep unhappiness. Many other professionals were offering sage advice about what to do about the problem. In fact, 'by 1962, the plight of the trapped American housewife had become a national parlor game' (Friedan, 1963). Such was the condescension with which the problem was being considered.

Educators and doctors, psychologists and media mavens, all came at the puzzling issue within the existing paradigm of traditional femininity, showing a dedication to the prerequisite that a woman's place is in the home. This idea was considered unshakeably 'fact'. But Betty argued that perspective obliterated a real examination of the problem. If we take that as true, she said, the only problems we can identify 'are those that might disturb her adjustment as a housewife'. If we look at the problem from this perspective, 'career is a problem, education is a problem, political interest, even the very admission of women's intelligence and individuality is a problem'(Friedan 1963). But what if that initial 'fact' were not fact at all?

Friedan looked around at the many ways in which 'the problem' was discussed and the proposed solutions. She found that although it was being widely deliberated, 'almost everybody who talked about it found some superficial reason to dismiss it' (Friedan 1963). Some blamed incompetent repairmen, some 'too much PTA', some 'too much time chauffeuring kids around in the car'. Many experts (even educators themselves) held that the introduction of women's education was to blame, as they noted that 'more and more women had education, which naturally made them unhappy in their role as housewives' (Friedan 1963). The suggestion that women no longer be admitted to four-year colleges and universities was bandied about, since clearly women would not be needing four more years of intellectual development in their penultimate role as wife and mother. That kind of preparation would only leave them helplessly overqualified and frustrated, and so should be terminated.

Too Much Education?

'The feminine mystique has made higher education for women seem suspect, unnecessary and even dangerous' said Friedan. 'But I think that education, and only education, has saved, and can continue to save, American women from the greater dangers of the feminine mystique' (Friedan 1963). Her response to colleges that she believed had abandoned their mission to prepare women for anything more weighty than a load of laundry was a cry of outrage. 'Instead of educating women for the greater maturity required to participate in modern society – with all the problems, conflicts and hard work involved... they began educating them to "play the role of woman".' (Friedan 1963)

Friedan claimed that the intent of these new functional educators was not to help women think critically, question freely, ponder deeply, and explore widely – as she had so happily done at Smith – but to promote women's adjustment to a life lived solely within the world of home and children. One women's college had even devised the slogan, 'We are not educating women to be scholars; we are educating them to be wives and mothers' (Friedan 1963). As sex-directed educators gave up preparing women for a career or gainful occupation, the results were profound: 'girls seemed suddenly incapable of any ambition, any vision, any passion, except the pursuit of a wedding ring' (Friedan 1963).

Selling the Consumer Path to Bliss

As educators abandoned their mission of developing the minds of young women, marketing mavens simultaneously moved in to provide a new vision of womanhood. In her research, Betty uncovered reams of interviews and marketing surveys that offered undeniable proof of who, precisely, profited from turning feisty educated women into appliance-hugging housewives. 'Properly manipulated...American housewives can be given the sense of identity, purpose, creativity, the self-realization, even the sexual joy they lack – by the buying of things,' wrote Austrian-American psychologist Ernest Dichter (1907–1991), the acknowledged father of consumer motivational research (and an acolyte of

Freud). His bestselling book, *The Psychology of Everyday Living* (1947), contained chapters on 'The Magic of Soap', 'What Bread Means to You' and 'How to Be Happy While Cooking'.

Friedan was not prepared to accept this 'expert' point of view, and chose to dig more deeply into the 'proper manipulation' that Dichter was extolling. She explored the ways in which marketers psychologically upped the ante by injecting 'professional pride' into a woman's stultifying daily routine of cooking and cleaning, to 'emphasize her kingpin role in the family' (Friedan 1963).

Dichter not only instructed firms in how to sell to women, but also moulded the idea of the ideal woman in the guise of the feminine mystique. As Horowitz (2000) acknowledges, in *The Feminine Mystique* Friedan

> *'cogently told how Dichter worked to squelch women's independence, and how he set out to manipulate women's desires in order to increase sales. She also well understood how he used the language of science and professionalism to give women the illusion of achievement, how he promoted labour-saving methods that did little to relieve drudgery, and how he played on women's guilt over not being more perfect housekeepers.'*

The advertising gurus promised to make women better wives and mothers – sexier, younger, happier – with just one little product! It was not only a seductive promise, but a never-ending tantalizing bait, because as Friedan explained, 'those unfulfilled promises can keep her endlessly hungry for things' and, perhaps more importantly, 'keep her from ever knowing what she really needs or wants' (Friedan 1963).

Fig. 5 A typical 1960s advertisement aimed at housewives.

Blaming the Feminists

Home economists suggested 'realistic' preparation for high school girls, like workshops on home appliance maintenance and use.

A male columnist even joked in *Harper's Bazaar* (July 1960) that the problem could be solved by taking away woman's right to vote.

> *'In the pre-19th Amendment era, the American woman was placid, sheltered and sure of her role in American society. She left all the political decisions to her husband and he, in turn, left all the family decisions to her. Today a woman has to make both the family and the political decisions, and it's too much for her.'* (Friedan, 1963)

The solutions were all meant to help women acquiesce to their role as wife and mother: to be more malleable, more accepting, less palpably miserable.

> *'They got all kinds of advice from the growing armies of marriage and child-guidance counselors, psychotherapists, and armchair psychologists on how to adjust to their role as housewives. No other road to fulfillment was offered to American women in the middle of the twentieth century.'* (Friedan 1963)

The problem with women, claimed the experts, was that they just didn't realize how lucky they were. 'What if she isn't happy – does she think men are happy in this world? Does she really, secretly, still want to be a man? Doesn't she know yet how lucky she is to be a woman?' (Friedan 1963)

The real culprit leading women astray, these experts surmised, was feminism. That was the dangerous fantasy that made women believe they could do more and claim more in their lives. Feminism's deceitful promise that femininity could coexist with independence, equality and achievement was surely what was driving women mad.

Friedan Redefines the Problem

Friedan offered a completely different assessment of the problem afflicting American women. For starters, she disavowed the idea that the women who were experiencing the worst anguish were rebels or feminist firebrands; instead, they were the very women who had tried most ardently to be happy at home. These were the women who drank chalky Metrecal shakes three times a day to stay model-thin; who dutifully cut and stitched Simplicity patterns, making home sewing a million-dollar industry; who were patient wives and long-suffering mother chauffeurs.

> *'I think, in fact, that this is the first clue to the mystery: the problem cannot be understood in the generally accepted terms by which scientists have studied women, doctors have treated them, counselors have advised them, and writers have written about them. Women who suffer this problem in whom this voice is stirring, have lived their whole lives in the pursuit of feminine fulfillment.'* (Friedan, 1963)

Instead of focusing on ameliorative adjustment (like some educators) or on the pathology of women who were feeling dead inside in the confines of their pretty homes (like some psychologists), Betty reframed the problem. In doing so, she blew a hole through the accepted doctrine of the day – that a woman's femininity (and ultimate happiness) depended on an all-consuming focus on one's husband and children.

The real problem, Betty claimed, was a definition of femininity that was clawing out the souls of women.

> *'The feminine mystique says that the highest value and the only commitment for women is the fulfillment of their own femininity. It says the great mistake of Western culture, through most of its history, has been the undervaluation of this femininity. It says this femininity is so mysterious and intuitive and close to the creation and origin of life that man-made science may never be able to understand it...The mistake, says the mystique, the root of women's troubles in the past, is that women envied men, women tried to be like men, instead of accepting their own nature, which can find fulfillment only in sexual passivity, male domination, and nurturing maternal love.'* (Friedan 1963)

In short, added Friedan, 'The new image this mystique gives to American women is the old image: "Occupation: housewife"'.

Building the False Ideal

Friedan insisted that something strange had happened: this archaic, biologically-determined view of women had been manipulated to make 'certain concrete, finite domestic aspects of feminine existence...into a religion, a pattern by which all women must now live or deny their femininity'. This insight would be absorbed by feminists and feminist psychotherapists such as Susie Orbach, who have noted the enduring, rigid hold of 'the ideal woman' – and the cost to any woman refusing to be defined by this ideal.

Friedan was interested in how this rigid ideal had come to be agreed and fixed in place. She contrasted the historic necessity of women's domesticity with the mystique's contemporary psychological insistence upon it.

> *'The material details of life, the daily burden of cooking and cleaning, of taking care of the physical needs of husband and children – these did indeed define a woman's world a century ago when Americans were pioneers, and the American frontier lay in conquering the land... Now the American frontiers are of the mind, and of the spirit. Love and children and home are good, but they are not the whole world, even if most of the words now written for women pretend they are.'* (Friedan 1963)

Those were revolutionary words in the 1960s, but Friedan didn't stop with simply examining the confining view of femininity. Having defined the mystique, which insisted that femininity resides inescapably in the biological capacity of women, Friedan began to peel back layer after layer of the 'problem' to reveal what was really at the heart of the mystery. What was the true cause of women's desperation?

Friedan explains that her methods were like those of a reporter on the trail of a story, but this was no ordinary story. During her research, she found that the startling pattern that began to emerge, across a vast range of modern thought and life, 'defied not only the conventional image but basic psychological assumptions about women' (Friedan 1963). Many ideas that were said to be 'facts' about women were assumptions, which had been woven into the discourse of daily life and culture to such an extent that everyone believed them to be true.

Friedan's background in psychology and radical politics, coupled with her fierce intellect, led her to question the complicity of educators, the media, psychologists, religion, culture and even women themselves in the ascendance of the mystique. She also detected the whiff of capitalist exploitation behind the enterprise. 'Somehow, somewhere, someone must have figured out that women will buy more things if they are kept in the underused, nameless-yearning, energy-to-get-rid-of state of being housewives.' (Friedan 1963)

If Friedan was right, and if the things that she was learning in her interviews and uncovering in her research were real, the implications were profound.

> *'It meant that I and every other woman I knew had been living a lie, and all the doctors who treated us and the experts who studied us were perpetuating that lie, and our homes and schools and churches and politics and professions were built around that lie.'* (Friedan 1963)

But was the mystique the cause of that underlying lie, or simply contributing to its powerful and insidious influence?

Why Had Women Retreated?

In *The Feminine Mystique*, Friedan was determined to confront 'the real mystery: why did so many American women, with the ability and education to discover and create, go back home again?' Why had women changed tack from the path that was beginning to be laid down by the First-Wave feminists, whose testimonies spoke of how their dangerous protests nonetheless made them feel 'so alive'?

Friedan challenged that wholesale retreat and its corrosive effect on women's psyche, asking, 'What happens when women try to live according to an image that makes them deny their minds? What happens when women grow up in an image that makes them deny the reality of the changing world?' (Friedan 1963) She answered those queries with an assertion that was not being voiced by any of the experts of the time.

Brick by brick, Betty set out her argument that women were being fed a false narrative about femininity and fulfillment, and they were suffering from it. After she typed out the book's first two chapters, she went home to her living room couch, hauled out her yellow legal pad, and in long-hand began to write her own truth. She explored her sense of unworthiness to pursue a 'real' career as a doctoral candidate in psychology. She commiserated with the pressure she felt to disavow her highest ambitions, fearing it would cost her her femininity (or her husband). And she challenged women to confront their ultimate human responsibility – to develop one's own identity.

The Problem is Identity

Friedan's conclusion was radical and revealing.

> *'It is my thesis that the core of the problem for women today is...a problem of identity – a stunting or evasion of growth that is perpetuated by the feminine mystique. It is my thesis that...our culture does not permit women to accept or gratify their basic need to grow and fulfill their potentialities as human beings.'* (Friedan 1963)

Methodically, meticulously, she set out the genesis and underpinnings of the mystique as well as the influences of the first feminists, and significant voices like Sigmund Freud, Margaret Mead, Erik Erikson and Abraham Maslow. Yet had she only described the problem, the desperation, and the yearning that women were feeling, the book would not have had the impact it did. What made *The Feminine Mystique* so powerful was that it reframed the problem and also promised a different solution.

As Hennessee (1999) points out: 'Betty explained that the system was crazy, women were not – that the current definition of femininity was wrong and...they were...not just somebody's daughter, wife or mother; they had an identity of their own.'

In pivoting away from the cultural and psychological conclusions that women were suffering from too much 'freedom' and simply needed to adjust to their natural feminine roles as wives and mothers, Friedan had to challenge both current and historical accepted truths.

> *'Women were being blamed for all kinds of 'problems' then – their children's bedwetting, their husbands' ulcers, not cleaning the kitchen sink white enough, not pressing their husbands' shirts smooth enough, their own lack of orgasm. But the 'problem' they kept bringing up... had nothing to do with children, marriage, home, sex.'* (Friedan 2000)

Women who had dutifully married at 20, had babies, baked a thousand meatloaves, and taken excellent care of their home and families found themselves feeling emptier than ever, with literally nothing to do except refold the towels or take a Valium. Perhaps, Betty wrote, the crisis wasn't in women's insufficient adjustment, it was in the very concept of what a woman might be and do with her life. It was, in Erik Erikson's words, a true identity crisis. 'A baked potato is not as big as the world and vacuuming the living room floor—with or without makeup—is not work that takes enough thought or energy to challenge any woman's full capacity.' (Friedan 1963)

It was Betty's contention that with the mystique, women were being told and sold a version of femininity that precluded the possibility of real growth, a striving for identity, and full maturity. Women were not the second-class thing that could only be explained in relation to that 'norm' that is the male. As Beauvoir had suggested, it is in seeing women only as the Other to man, rather than either the norm or a different kind of being in her own right, that she effectively disappears. Friedan suggested that we need to stop seeing women in terms of family roles and allow her centre stage. Then she would be free to begin to find an identity and seek the same path of individual growth and development that was, in the 1960s, already being offered to men. 'The expectations of feminine fulfillment ... operate as a kind of youth serum, keeping most women in the state of sexual larvae, preventing them from achieving the maturity of which they are capable.' (Friedan 1963)

Women of the 1950s and 60s, Friedan contended, were victims of a false-belief system that required them to find identity through others (their husbands and children). She suggested that women needed to be freed up to step out of that belief system, and so forge an identity for themselves.

They were unable to do this for many reasons, according to Friedan. But one of the strongest ways in which they were held back was the absolute ridicule and humiliation that had rained down on the First-Wave feminists. The mystique wasn't simply wrong- minded thinking. It also represented a specific and targeted repudiation and rejection of the courageous example of the first feminists, and their 'vilified, misinterpreted journey away from home' (Friedan 1963).

Learning from the Attacks on the First Wave

In exploring the first women's rights movement, Friedan was clearly full of admiration for the early pioneers and enraged by the lack of respect given to their battle. It had been only 40 years earlier – after a century of protesting, fighting and rebelling – that American women had literally changed the trajectory of society by getting the vote, earning legal recognition, insisting upon the right to an education, and demanding equality. Yet where was the sense of awe and attribution?

> *'It has been popular in recent years to laugh at feminism as one of history's dirty jokes: to pity, sniggering, those old-fashioned feminists who fought for women's rights to higher education, careers, the vote. They were neurotic victims of penis envy; they denied their very nature as women, which fulfills itself only through sexual passivity, acceptance of male domination, and nurturing motherhood.'* (Friedan, 1963)

The more she researched, the more Friedan realized that 'every step of the way, [the first wave] feminists had to fight the conception that they were violating the God-given nature of woman' (Friedan 1963). The Bible was very clear in its insistence that man was dominant, and woman was subservient, because 'the head of every woman is man'. Here was an authority that could be called upon by men for insisting on women's compliance: 'Let your women be silent in the churches, for it is not permitted unto them to speak...And if they will learn anything, let them ask their husbands at home' (Friedan 1963).

Friedan decided to research the writings of the First-Wave feminists herself, to find out if they really were the strange, grim beings that their commonly accepted image foretold. Given all the opposition and opprobrium they had met with – from government, religion, society and male commentators from many quarters – she expected this to be something like the case. And yet, when she actually turned to the diaries and letters of those early feminists, she learned about the invigorating, enhancing, purposeful and joyful lives they had led while pursuing their cause. These intelligent, witty and brave women described the extraordinary sensation of working together to achieve something they passionately believed in. Their lives had meaning,

Fig. 6 First-Wave suffragists travelling to Boston to protest, c.1910.

and in turn, they felt fully alive. In advocating for themselves and feeling their own power and capacity for self-actualization, far from shrivelling up and wilting, the early feminists, Friedan found, 'cast off the shadow of contempt and self-contempt that had degraded women for centuries' (Friedan 1963).

The First-Wave feminists gloried in their abilities, their strength and their sense of freedom and purpose. They were not weak.

> *'In their own lifetime, such women changed the feminine image that had justified woman's degradation. At a meeting while men jeered at trusting the vote to woman so helpless that they had to be lifted over mud puddles and handed into carriages, a proud feminist named Sojourner Truth raised her black arm: "Look at my arm! I have ploughed and planted and gathered into barns... and ain't I a woman? I could work as much and eat as much as a man—when I could get it—and bear the lash as well...I have borne 13 children and seen most of 'em sold into slavery, and when I cried out with my mother's grief, none but Jesus helped me—and ain't I a woman?"'* (Friedan 1963)

Unquestionably, the revolution that was the women's movement threatened the status and position of men. Feminists demanding the right to education, to vote, to own property, were social reformers committed to changing the cultural, sexual and economic injustices they saw around them, and the usual forces of reaction lined up against them, intent upon denigrating and destroying their credibility.

> *'It is a strangely unquestioned perversion of history that the passion and fire of the feminist movement came from man-hating, embittered, sex-starved spinsters, from castrating, unsexed non-women who burned with such envy for the male organ that they wanted to take it away from all men, or destroy them, demanding rights only because they lacked the power to love as women.'* (Friedan 1963)

The Myth of the Man-eating Feminist

But while Elizabeth Cady Stanton, Julia Ward Howe and others blazed a trail for women's rights and won the vote, they left precious few footsteps for successive generations of women to follow. While those ardent feminists were successful in earning emancipation,

> *'they could not erase the hostility, the prejudice, the discrimination that still remained. Nor could they paint the new image of what women might become when they grew up under conditions that no longer made them inferior to men, dependent, passive, incapable of thought or decision.'* (Friedan 1963)

Into that vacuum, reappeared the 'myth of the man-eating feminist which is prevalent today, a myth that has cropped up continuously ... whenever anyone has reason to oppose women's move out of the home' (Friedan 1963). Plenty of businessmen, religions, psychologists, politicians, husbands and fathers had plenty of reasons to want to keep women at home, and together they fanned the flames of the mystique into a bonfire.

The first feminists' battle had been focused on legal rights and representation, and when these had been won, women were free to be whatever they chose. 'But what choice were they offered?' asks Friedan. 'In that corner, the fiery, man-eating feminist, the career woman – loveless, alone. In this corner, the gentle wife and mother – loved and protected by her husband, surrounded by her adoring children.' (Friedan 1963) How is this a free choice? Is it any wonder, she queries, that the mystique caught up so many women in its spell?

The Pain of Change

An identity crisis – which is how Friedan characterized the 'problem with no name' of the 1950s and 60s – is not an easy thing to work through. Erikson, who had coined the phrase, compared it to a second birth, with all the attendant labour pains and trauma. Truly, the search for one's independent identity can be disorienting and anxiety-ridden, he said, yet it is necessary for maturity.

Friedan likened women's condition, post First-Wave feminism, to that of Chinese women whose feet had been bound, but were finally free. The pain of those unbound feet must surely have been excruciating, she said, as the bones expanded and began to grow. After such harsh compression, some women were afraid to stand, let alone to walk or run.

> *'But what would have happened if, before a single generation of Chinese girls had grown up with unbound feet, doctors, hoping to save them pain and distress, told them to bind their feet again? And teachers told them that walking with bound feet was feminine, the only way a woman could walk if she wanted a man to love*

> *her? And scholars told them that they would be better mothers if they could not walk too far away from their children? And peddlers, discovering that women who could not walk brought more trinkets, spread fables of the dangers of running and the bliss of being bound?'* (Friedan 1963)

Although feminists had won legal and voting rights for women, they hadn't worked out a new way of being in the world. They hadn't suggested what this new woman might look like, or do. Friedan suggested that the pain of freedom without a vision of identity was so great, that when society wanted to push women back into the home after the war (to give jobs back to men), they did so by offering an 'empowered version of femininity (housework and motherhood, gilded with affluence and gadgets)'. And women, wary of stepping into an unknown abyss, gracefully accepted the deal, turning their back on the hard work of forging an identity.

Just as a bound foot may be familiar but still compromises one's ability to walk and run, the feminine mystique was just pretty icing on the same old patriarchal cake. Friedan used Maslow's theory of self-actualization to prophesize,

> *'The feminine mystique has succeeded in burying millions of American women alive. Only by… a personal commitment to the future can American women break out of the housewife trap and truly find fulfillment as wives and mothers—by fulfilling their own unique possibilities as separate human beings.'* (Friedan 1963)

The Solution, According to Friedan

In *The Feminine Mystique*, Friedan finally and fulsomely articulates her solution to 'the problem that has no name', while addressing the fear and resistance voiced by the thousands of women she had spoken to across America. She exhorts her sisters to literally work through it – to get an education and paid professional work that challenges their abilities. 'The feminists saw clearly that education and the right to participate in the more advanced work of society were women's greatest needs.' (Friedan 1963)

She anticipates the hostile husband, the envious other housewives, women's inner guilt and ambivalence about their own ambitions, and answers it all with this empowering admonition: 'The only way for a woman, as for a man, to find herself, to know herself as a person, is by creative work of her own.' (Friedan 1963)

Friedan's belief in meaningful, paid work, in education, and in a woman's essential worth, flowed like a river through her entire life and informs her counsel to her readers. Her faith in women's ability led her to this hopeful query: 'Who knows what women's intelligence will contribute when it can be nourished?' (Friedan 1963) The possibilities were literally boundless.

Long-lasting Influence

The Feminine Mystique changed Betty Friedan's life. She re-lit the fire of feminism because she didn't hold back on what she knew to be true, in her own life and in five years of researching, interviewing, questioning, puzzling over, and attacking women's repression. And she wouldn't shut up about it, not in her book nor in the next 40 years of her life as she advocated for a humanist American awakening. In *The Feminine Mystique* she wove together her own personal narrative with hundreds of authentic voices to create a tapestry of women longing to create a new reality and richer possibilities for themselves. And she exhorted and empowered them to do it.

The Feminine Mystique and the movement it ignited had a profound influence on American culture. Millions of women read the book and quite literally went out and changed their lives, just as Friedan had challenged them to do. And that changed America in the process.

What Came of it All?

Consider the statistics. In 1960, women – married or single – could not get a credit card in their own name. In most states of the USA, they could not serve on a jury because women were considered too fragile to hear disturbing testimony, and too emotional to render a verdict. Women, married or single, were barred from using the birth control pill as a contraceptive. No matter how intelligent, women could not attend Harvard, Yale, Princeton, Brown or Dartmouth. They could be fired from a job for being pregnant. And they earned just 59 cents for every dollar a man earned in a similar job.

By 1970, 80 per cent of American wives were using contraception and in control of their own reproduction. In the next decade, abortion would be constitutionally protected and the long struggle to pass the Equal Rights Amendment would begin. Women would run for political office, enter the work force in record numbers, and unapologetically seek the corner office. By 1976, *The Feminine Mystique* would seem almost quaint, as *Time* magazine awarded its 'Man of the Year' cover to 'American Women'.

The introductory accolade reads like a Betty Friedan fantasy:

> *'They have arrived like a new immigrant wave in male America. They may be cops, judges, military officers, telephone linemen, cab drivers, pipefitters, editors, business executives—or mothers and housewives, but not quite the same subordinate creatures they were before. Across the broad range of American life, from suburban tract houses to state legislatures, from church pulpits to Army barracks, women's lives are profoundly changing, and with them, the traditional relationships between the sexes. ...1975 was not so much the Year of the Woman as the Year of the Women—an immense variety of women altering their lives, entering new fields, functioning with a new sense of identity, integrity and confidence.'* (*Time* magazine, 5 January 1976)

In the same article, newspaper critic Elizabeth Janeway took up Friedan's call, saying: 'The sky above us lifts, the light pours in. No maps exist for this enlarged world. We must make them as we explore.'

4. Friedan Vs. Freud

Ever since Friedan had stumbled across psychology as a teenager, it had been a powerfully guiding force in her life. Her natural talent led her to become a summa cum laude psychology student in college and a doctoral candidate in the field. She also turned to psychoanalytic therapy repeatedly throughout her life to cope with her crippling asthma. So it is not surprising that in the years of research leading to her master work, she was driven to 'get behind the façade of the feminine mystique, to dig out its origins and the base of its appeal...to dig deep into my intellectual roots in psychology' (Friedan 2000).

The deeper she dug, the more she hit the same vein of belief that was starkly Freudian in nature. 'It is a Freudian idea, hardened into apparent fact, that has trapped so many American women today' (Friedan 1963) she stated. And nothing could express that Freudian idea more succinctly than his famous quote, 'Anatomy is destiny'.

Context is Critical

The idea that 'anatomy is destiny' first appeared in Freud's 1912 essay 'On the Universal Tendency to Debasement in the Sphere of Love'. Interestingly, he was paraphrasing another titan not known for his humility – Napoleon Bonaparte – and the statement was not originally intended to suggest that a person's gender determines his or her primary personality traits and life possibilities. Instead, Freud was contending that sexuality will always be disappointing. First, because the true and longed-for love object, the mother, is not involved, and second, because a human's sexual apparatus is not very aesthetically pleasing. Here is the complete quote:

> *'One might say here, varying a well-known saying of the great Napoleon: 'Anatomy is destiny.' The genitals themselves have not taken part in the development of the human body in the direction of beauty: they have remained animal, and thus love, too, has remained in essence just as animal as it ever was.'* (Freud 1912)

Given the thrust of Freud's other work and writings about women, it is understandable that the quote has been widely cited to make the case for women's inescapable inferiority (in lacking a penis) and to insist that their biological destiny is to be, first and foremost, the bearers of children. Friedan had been studying Freud since her college days at Smith, and by the age of 37, she was immersed in Freudian ideology – in particular, the seminal concepts of castration fantasy and penis envy that he believed defined the psychology of men and women. Although Friedan duly acknowledged that 'Freud's discovery of the unconscious workings of the mind was one of the great breakthroughs in man's pursuit of knowledge' (Friedan 1963), she also believed that Freudian thought had created a resolute ideology that women were defined by what they were not (a man), and therefore differed from the 'standard' or norm. As a result, women were seen as – and believed themselves to be – trapped in a passive, shadow role that prohibited growth and the development of an independent identity.

Friedan bemoaned the fact that Freudian theory had been twisted to 'become the ideological bulwark of the sexual counter-revolution in America', a force insisting that women's only true fulfillment lay in motherhood and the home. Without a doubt, Freudian doctrine dominated American culture in the 1950s. 'It would be half-wrong to say it started with Sigmund Freud. It did not really start, in America, until the 1940s. And then again, it was less a start than the prevention of an end.' (Friedan 1963)

So, what and who did create the feminine mystique? Friedan places the blame on the messengers of society, who spread Freudian ideas through media and educational institutions:

> *'It was the creation of writers and editors in the mass media, ad-agency motivation researchers, and behind them the popularizers and translators of Freudian thought in the colleges and universities. Freudian and pseudo- Freudian theories settled everywhere, like fine volcanic ash... Sociology, anthropology, education, even the study of history and literature became permeated and transfigured by Freudian thought.'* (Friedan 1963)

The Freudian Mystique

The Freudian ideology that was bandied around in the 1940s was not always taken from actual Freudian theory, Friedan pointed out, and she was careful not to dismiss psychoanalysis in principle. Originally, she claimed, 'Freudian psychology, with its emphasis on freedom from a repressive morality to achieve sexual fulfillment, was part of the ideology of women's emancipation' (Friedan 1963). However, when this idea jumped from the page and real, living women began to chain themselves to fences, protest, demand the vote, seek paid work and fend for themselves, Freud's more Victorian postulations about the cause of neuroses in women somehow took on hefty contemporary relevance. Western societies in the 1950s and 60s, including America, fell back onto Freudian notions of female neurosis. It was, in short, a long look backwards.

> *'Without Freud's definition of the sexual nature of woman to give the conventional image of femininity new authority, I do not think several generations of educated, spirited American women would have been so easily diverted from the dawning realization of who they were and what they could be.'* (Friedan 1963)

In addition, as Friedan noted, this idea was given more weight because the voices of science and education were behind the new mystique, making it that much more difficult for women to challenge, combat or even recognize. Especially so, she says, for women who had studied science at college and university. Their place within the scientific community ensured compliance with its conventional views.

However, while women accepted the 'scientific' backing for the idea that biological factors determined destiny, they – like the media and educational institutions who preached the doctrine of endangered femininity – were unaware of its Freudian origin.

But there it was, hiding beneath a façade that glorified timid, tender, always-threatened and never-threatening femininity: the Freudian concept of woman's inherent inferiority. And this idea had far-reaching consequences, damning women to being 'less than' men in every conceivable way. Friedan noted that it served to prop up 'the old prejudices—women are animals, less than human, unable to think like men, born merely to breed and serve men'. This idea of women's 'natural inferiority' had been challenged by the First-Wave feminists of the 19th century, but its enduring strength and resurgence in the 1950s showed that it was 'not so easily dispelled by the crusading feminists, by science and education, and by the democratic spirit after all' (Friedan 1963).

Friedan, however, refused to accept the idea that women are naturally inferior, or that they exist only to bear and care for children. She decided to return to the source of these ideas and challenge the theories of Freud himself. Psychology has grown and developed hugely as a discipline since Freud's time, she noted, adding that 'I think much of the Freudian theory about women is obsolescent', in the same way that it had been surpassed in many areas of psychology. What's more, she said, it is 'an obstacle to truth for women in America today, and a major cause of the pervasive problem that has no name' (Friedan 1963). The problem is not that women are defying a natural (biologically determined) femininity, or 'feminine mystique', Friedan claimed, but that in trying to fit into it, this old-fashioned idea of femininity was crippling them. While modern psychology sought ways to help men to find greater self-actualization and a true sense of self, it explicitly denied this to women, looking backwards to Freudian ideas and fixed notions of what a woman 'should be'.

Penis Envy or Longing for Fair Competition?

In challenging Freudian ideas about women, Friedan realized that she would have to challenge the entire theory of 'penis envy', first suggested by Freud in 1908, in his paper 'On the Sexual Theories of Children'. Expanding on the idea in 1925, he said of girls:

> *'They notice the penis of a brother or playmate, strikingly visible and of large proportions, at once recognize it as the superior counterpart of their own small and inconspicuous organ, and from that time forward fall a victim to envy for the penis.'* (Freud 1925)

Friedan notes that Freud saw this as an expansion of his Oedipal Complex in boys, which included the idea that boys suffer a Castration Complex as a result of seeing female genitals for the first time. From that time onwards, boys suffer from castration- anxiety, according to Freud, and this is a motivation for psychological development. Turning his attention to girls, Freud assumed that they also undergo a Castration Complex. Upon seeing male genitals for the first time, says Freud in his lecture 'The Psychology of Women', a girl

> *'immediately notices the difference, and, it must be admitted, its significance. She feels herself at a great disadvantage, and often declares that she would like to have something like that too and falls a victim to penis-envy, which leaves ineradicable traces on her development and character-formation.'* (Freud 1929)

Friedan notes that whereas Freud sees this as a useful complex in a boy's development, it can have a disastrous effect on girls who are not only envious, but apparently (according to Freud) refuse to give up their desire for this anatomical feature.

> *'"The discovery of her castration is a turning-point in the life of the girl", Freud went on to say. "She is wounded in her self-love by the unfavourable comparison with the boy, who is so much better equipped." ... This either leads to complete sexual inhibition and neurosis, or to a "masculinity complex" in which she refuses to give up "phallic" activity (that is, "activity such as is usually characteristic of the male").'* (Friedan, quoting Freud 1963)

In 1925, Freud had suggested that in a girl, penis envy constituted a 'wound to her narcissism' and that 'she develops, like a scar, a sense of inferiority'. In addition, he added, even after 'penis envy has abandoned its true object, it continues to exist: by an easy displacement it persists in the character trait of jealousy'. He goes on to say that 'critics of every epoch' have found that 'women show less sense of justice than men, that they are less ready to submit to the great exigencies of life, that they are more often influenced in their judgments by feelings of affection or hostility' and that all of these 'truths' about women are due to the problem of penis envy.

Perhaps sensing the less-than-solid ground on which he was theorizing, and jumping from his theory in order to tie in 'the old prejudices' as scientific fact, Freud continues, 'We must not allow ourselves to be deflected from such conclusions by the denials of the feminists'. Betty Friedan picked up this gauntlet and decided to look at the whole idea of penis envy from the other end of the telescope – from the point of view of a woman, rather than a man's conjecture about what they believe might be happening in girls and women.

Friedan's Perspective on 'Penis Envy'

Friedan credits Freud with noticing that women were envious about men in some way, but she questioned what that envy revolved around. 'What was Freud really reporting?' she asked.

> *'If one interprets "penis envy" as other Freudian concepts have been reinterpreted, in the light of our new knowledge that what Freud believed to be biological was often a cultural reaction, one sees simply that Victorian culture gave women many reasons to envy men: the same conditions, in fact, that the feminists fought against.'* (Friedan 1963)

Given that Freud was so adept in seeing the symbolic ways in which things might be used in dreams or artistic works, it is strange that he took the occasional appearance of a woman with a penis in these scenarios quite literally. Friedan says,

> *'If a woman who was denied the freedom, the status, and the pleasures that men enjoyed wished secretly that she could have these things, in the shorthand of the dream, she might wish herself a man and see herself with that one thing which made men unequivocally different—the penis. …If she secretly despised herself, and envied man for all she was not, she might go through the motions of love, or even feel a slavish adoration, but would she be capable of free and joyous love? You cannot explain away woman's envy of man, or her contempt for herself, as mere*

> *refusal to accept her sexual deformity, unless you think that a woman, by nature, is a being inferior to man. Then, of course, her wish to be equal is neurotic.'* (Friedan 1963)

More Freudian Fuel for the Fire

How did Freud's view of women, beyond 'penis envy', influence American thinking? Friedan contends he saw them 'as childlike dolls, who existed in terms only of man's love, to love man and serve his needs'. To Freud, men and women were like the sun and planets (with man at the centre, of course). 'It was the same kind of unconscious solipsism that made man for many centuries see the sun only as a bright object that revolved around the Earth' (Friedan, 1963). Freud simply couldn't see beyond the paradigm in which he lived.

Friedan explores how in his own life, Freud beheld evidence of this heliocentric theory, as his mother 'seemed to exist only to gratify his every wish', while his sisters – and later his wife – built households that revolved completely around him. His mother worshipped him, and even his sisters' beloved piano disappeared from the family home after Sigmund complained to his parents that the music was interrupting his studies. The idea that women were mere handmaids to men was not troubling to Freud; indeed, he saw it as the natural order. He took the daily evidence of his society and culture to represent eternal truths. As Betty explains: 'Freud did not see this as a problem, or cause for any problem, in women. It was woman's nature to be ruled by man and her sickness to envy him' (Friedan 1963). It seemed that everywhere he looked, he found more apparent reasons to back up the idea that a woman's desire for equality was a 'sickness' and the breaking of a 'natural' law.

In *The Feminine Mystique*, Friedan was investigating the lives and feelings of affluent housewives, so she examined Freud's own marriage, too. She discovered Freud's ideas were entirely Victorian, as revealed in letters he wrote to his 'sweet child' and young fiancée Martha during their four-year engagement. 'I know, after all, how sweet you are, how you can turn a house into a paradise, how you will share *in my interests*.' [Author's italics.] Anticipating their natural division of labour, he proposes, 'I will let you rule the house as much as you wish, and you will reward me with your sweet love' (Friedan, 1963). The proposed bargain, it seemed, was that the male would be kind enough to let the woman 'rule the house' and the woman would gratefully repay with him with 'sweet love'. It seems not to have occurred to Freud that a woman with her own income might be in a different negotiating position – but how could he foresee that women might one day be given full access to the world of work and independent income?

And yet, there were people – men and women – even before Freud's time who defended female emancipation, such as John Stuart Mill, the famous humanist philosopher. In answer to Mill's call for gender equality, Freud said,

> *'If ... I imagined my gentle sweet girl as a competitor, it would only end in my telling her, as I did 17 months ago, that I am fond of her and that I implore her to withdraw from the strife into the calm, uncompetitive activity of my home... It is really a stillborn thought to send women into the struggle for existence exactly as man.'* (Friedan, 1963)

Why Freud Was Wrong

Freud spent his career working to understand neurotic women in Vienna at the turn of the 20th century, and Friedan freely admits he 'was a most perceptive and accurate observer of important problems of the human personality. But in describing and interpreting those problems, he was a prisoner of his own culture' (Friedan, 1963).

What Freud observed, listened to, and uncovered – which he believed to be universal and timeless truths – was actually only true for those particular people living in that particular place and time. Freud could not see the full picture, nor could he have predicted how growing cultural awareness and the concept of relativity would challenge 'the strict determinism that characterized the scientific thinking of the Victorian era' (Friedan 1963). Friedan draws our attention to comparing the world of Freud and her own in the 1960s: 'One needs only to know what Freud was describing, in those Victorian women, to see the fallacy in literally applying his theory of femininity to women today' (Friedan 1963). Entrenched Freudian concepts like 'anatomy is destiny' have become obsolete, Friedan argued, because 'Determinism has been replaced today by a more complex view of cause and effect, in terms of physical processes and phenomena as well as psychological' (Friedan 1963).

Friedan quoted the eminent psychoanalyst Clara Thompson, who revered Freud but also challenged his lack of cultural context when exploring women's psychology:

> *'He accepted as an inevitable part of the fate of being a woman the limitation of outlook and life of the Victorian era... The castration complex and penis*

> *envy concepts, two of the most basic ideas in his whole thinking, are postulated on the assumption that women are biologically inferior to men.'* (Friedan 1963)

This underlying assumption of female inferiority Friedan identified as the cudgel driving home the feminine mystique.

It is in calling forth these time-specific ideas, generalizing them into 'natural laws' and forcing them onto every woman in every culture that enables still-patriarchal societies to label women 'neurotic' if they fail to obey those laws. The women of America in her own era, Friedan says, were actually being expected to conform to Victorian standards, but this was not obvious because women were concurrently being told that their destiny relied on their biology, and as a 'law of nature', that would never change. Therefore, women's desires and inferiorities, as suggested with authority by Freud, would also never change.

> *'The concepts that gave the feminine mystique its intellectual authority distorted and twisted a particular time-and culture-bound phenomenon into a universal, ineradicable, permanent, biologically determined destiny, perpetuating the inferior housewife woman in Victorian Vienna, reincarnated in the glorified suburban housewife of post-World War II America.'* (Friedan 2000)

Despite the advances in understanding that psychological theories are just theories – not gospel and not immutable fact – somehow Freudian theory was elevated into a scientific religion in 1950s America. And educators, magazine editors and the general public believed in this 'scientific religion'. They bought it. They just couldn't understand why it was making women so desperately unhappy, to the point of wishing they could die.

> *'In the light of our new knowledge of cultural processes and of human growth, one would assume that women who grew up with the rights and freedom and education that Victorian women were denied would be different from the women Freud tried to cure...But Freud was interpreted to American women in such curiously literal terms that the concept of penis envy acquired a mystical life of its own, as if it existed quite independent of the women in whom it had been observed...Freud's Victorian image of woman became more real than the 20th-century women to whom it was applied.'* (Friedan 1963)

First-Wave Backlash

The era following World War II was uniquely fashioned for the Freudian message to resonate deeply. The postwar period was dubbed 'The Age of Anxiety' by the British- American poet W.H. Auden for good reason. 'After the loneliness of war and the unspeakableness of the bomb, against the frightening uncertainty, the cold immensity of the changing world, women as well as men sought the comforting reality of home and children.' (Friedan 1963)

Amidst all the insecurity and existential dread, home and family became the very nexus of national security. And who was responsible for ensuring the continued existence of those bulwark institutions? Women, naturally – and with great responsibility came the opportunity for great blame.

A Focal Point for all of Society's Ills

Bolstered by Freudian theory, study after study revealed that mothers were the primary cause of all the inchoate anxiety and ennui in post-war American society. Specifically, women working outside the home, women 'selfishly' wanting careers, women being insufficiently devoted to their husbands and children, women ruining sex with their over- educated brains.

> *'By unfortunate coincidence, this attack against mothers came almost at the same time that American women had just begun to use the rights of their emancipation, to go in increasing numbers to college and professional schools, to rise in industry and the professions in inevitable competition with men.'* (Friedan 1963)

Despite the fact that these young women couldn't possibly be the mothers of the troubled postwar generation, 'all the neuroses of children past and present were blamed on the independence and individuality of this new generation of American girls' (Friedan 1963).

It is difficult to overstate the intensity of the message, nor the perils to family and children articulated by trusted social scientists analyzing American culture through a Freudian lens.

> *'Accordingly, American neo-Freudians substituted anxiety for sex as the underlying cause of psychological maladies. They replaced Freudian tropes with a focus on family dynamics, especially the need for emotional security in early childhood. Mothers bore the brunt of this new diagnostic scrutiny: overprotective mothers*

> *stunted their children's maturation and were, according to a leading American psychiatrist, "our gravest menace" in the fight against communism; excessively permissive mothers produced children who would become juvenile delinquents; a mother who smothered a son with affection risked making him homosexual, while the undemonstrative "refrigerator mother" was blamed for what is now diagnosed as autism.'* (Groopman 2019)

Or as Friedan simply stated, 'It was suddenly discovered that the mother could be blamed for almost everything.' (Friedan 1963).

With this new emphasis on women as Atlas – not merely holding up half the sky, as in the Chinese proverb, but now solely responsible for the mental health of the entire nation – small wonder that women retreated from the workplace to devote themselves entirely to preventing neuroses in their families by their daily devotion.

> *'Freud was accepted so quickly and completely at the end of the forties that for over a decade no one even questioned the race of the educated American woman back to the home. When questions finally had to be asked...they were asked so completely within the Freudian framework that only one answer was possible: education, freedom, rights are wrong for women.'* (Friedan 1963)

No Way Out

Freud had contended that even if times changed drastically and women did go out in the world to earn a livelihood like men, requiring '...changes in upbringing [to] suppress all a woman's tender attributes...' that anatomy would still trump ambition. No legal reforms would alter the fact that women do not have the physical attributes, in Freud's opinion, that were necessary to live a full, independent life: 'All reforming action in law and education would break down in front of the fact that, long before the age at which a man can earn a position in society, Nature has determined woman's destiny through beauty, charm and sweetness.' (Friedan 1963)

Friedan realized something tragic – that while Freudian thought had freed men from the tyranny of the past, weirdly, his 'anatomy is destiny' theory continued to 'chain women to an old image, [that] prohibits choice and growth, and denies them individual identity' (Friedan 1963).

It's all About Sex, But...

Sexuality was the focus of all Freud's theories, and certainly Freud saw women only in terms of their sexual relationship to men. So Friedan asked – is that all there is?

> *'It is recognized now that Freud never gave proper attention, even in man, to growth of the ego or self: "the impulse to master, control or come to self-fulfilling terms with the environment". Analysts who have freed themselves from Freud's bias and joined other behavioral scientists in studying the human need to grow, are beginning to believe that this is the basic human need, and that interference with it, in any dimension, is the source of psychic trouble.'* (Friedan 1963)

Instead of penis envy, Friedan pointed to this lack of support for growth, and the ensuing lack of full identity development, as the cause of women's suffering. It was only because women and femininity were examined through a Freudian, biologically constricted lens, that the real truth had been concealed, she argued. Freud had sought 'scientific' evidence to back up his existing ideas, rather than starting from an open- minded position. 'When [Freud] dismissed woman's yearning for equality as "penis envy," was he not merely stating his own view that women could never really be man's equal?' (Friedan, 1963)

Friedan demanded an update.

> *'Even if Freud and his contemporaries considered women inferior by God- given, irrevocable nature, science does not justify such a view today... when women's equal intelligence has been proved... their equal capacity in every sphere... demonstrated... a theory explicitly based on woman's natural inferiority would seem as ridiculous as it is hypocritical.'* (Friedan 1963)

Maslow Vs. the Mystique

For a more humanistic modern psychological perspective, Friedan turned to the American psychologist Abraham Maslow. Born into a family of New York Russian Jews in 1908, Maslow had studied with the Freudian psychotherapist Alfred Adler but soon developed his own original psychological concepts based on the study of mentally healthy and highly accomplished people, rather than concentrating solely on those experiencing difficulties in mental health. In other words, he focused on people's positive qualities, eschewing Freud's relentless focus on neuroses. Maslow argued that most people have a strong desire to reach their full potential, a level of 'self- actualization'. His famous 'hierarchy of needs' (which was only later depicted by others as a pyramid) was constructed to illustrate that basic material needs – food, water, sleep, safety, shelter – must be satisfied before one can aspire to achieve, to live up to one's full potential, and to experience states of peace, beauty, understanding, wholeness and serenity.

Friedan fervently embraced humanistic psychology and became close friends with Maslow while researching *The Feminine Mystique.* She believed that women trapped in permanent domesticity and a life of tireless service to their children and husbands were being systematically denied the opportunity to become fully human, self-actualized and happy. Succinctly claiming, 'our culture does not permit women to accept or gratify their basic need to grow and fulfill their potentialities as human beings' (Friedan 1963), she set out to enlighten and empower women to rise.

Despite the fact that '...the very nature of Freudian thought makes it virtually invulnerable to question' (Friedan 1963), she was bold enough to make the case. Step one was eschewing the backward-looking Freudian picture of the perfectly subservient wife and mother, utterly fulfilled by her homely chores.

> *'Girls who grew up playing baseball, baby-sitting, mastering geometry almost independent enough, almost resourceful enough, to meet the problems of the fission-fusion era—were told by the most advanced thinkers of our time to go back and live their lives as if they*

> *were Noras, restricted to the doll's house by Victorian prejudice. And their own respect and awe for the authority of science ...kept them from questioning the feminine mystique.'* (Friedan 1963)

The Freudian idea of the super-ego is that it functions to pass on entrenched ideas and cultural roles, '...and this Freudian super-ego worked for growing numbers of young and impressionable American women as Freud said...to perpetuate the past' (Friedan 1963).

The idea that 'Anatomy is destiny' was an idea from the past, Friedan contended. It was time for a new perspective. Perhaps, she suggested, the most important part of a woman was her voice.

5. Awareness Without Action is Pointless

'It wasn't enough just to start a movement for women's rights. You had to make it happen.' (Friedan 2000)

Betty Friedan didn't set out to be an activist. She was a writer and psychology geek who became fascinated by a very particular phenomenon, and in following her instincts, wrote a book that made her suddenly and surprisingly famous. By 1964, the funny- looking girl from Peoria had undeniably made it big and was enjoying every dazzling minute of the talk shows, rapt audiences and interviewers seeking her opinion about the state of American women. Maybe it had never occurred to Friedan, while she was writing about women's need to liberate themselves, that she would have to put her mojo where her mouth was. Slowly but surely, however, the consciousness she had raised in other women spurred her on in ways she never could have imagined.

Friedan had been trying to figure out what to write about next, to take advantage of the interest swirling around her, but nothing quite gelled into a motivating or cohesive idea. 'I surely wasn't getting much of anywhere, looking for patterns beyond the feminine mystique,' remembered Friedan, 'there was all this talk, talk, talk about women and no action' (Friedan 2000).

A Movement is Born

But the times they were a changin'. In 1964, that anthemic song of Bob Dylan's was released. America declared war against North Vietnam. Race riots erupted in big cities, and the Civil Rights Law, banning racial segregation and sex discrimination, was passed. Three civil rights workers were murdered in Mississippi. Dr. Martin Luther King Jr. was awarded the Nobel Peace Prize. The Berkeley Free Speech movement began. People were waking up from the long somnolence of the conformist 50s, getting up off the sofa and moving into the streets.

The genesis of the women's movement occurred as a series of fortunate events and sidelong happenstance that brought galvanizing women into Friedan's orbit. In the airport after a conference, she met Marlene Sanders, one of the first women reporters on ABC television, who was fascinated by what Friedan was rambling on about, in her rapid-fire, gravelly voice. Muriel Fox, a powerful executive vice president in public relations, heard Friedan speak and wrote her a note after the meeting declaring, 'If you ever decide to start an NAACP [National Association for the Advancement of Colored People] for women, count me in.' Dr. Pauli Murray, a noted black lawyer and law professor at Yale Law School (who had anonymously typed some of Friedan's early manuscripts), gave Friedan her first heads-up of a huge opportunity to advance women's rights, through an unenforced provision in a law nobody expected to pass.

To Get Attention, Just Add Sex

In 1964, President Lyndon Johnson's epic Civil Rights Act was coming up for a vote in the House of Representatives. Howard Smith of Virginia, an ardent segregationist, hated the bill but was persuaded by the indefatigable Michigan Representative Martha Griffiths to add the word 'sex' to the Title VII list of prohibited employment discrimination categories (alongside race, colour, religion and national origin). Smith was so sure that the addition of 'sex' to the Title VII list would cause the entire act to fail, he agreed. Indeed, when the 'sex' provision of the bill was announced, the House broke out in hoots of jeering laughter. But thanks to the efforts of Griffiths and the Repubican politician Margaret Chase Smith of Maine, the only woman in the Senate, both chambers were shamed (and cajoled by President Johnson) into passing the legislation.

Title VII of the Civil Rights Act formally established the Equal Employment Opportunity Commission (EEOC) to enforce sex discrimination protection, and that was Pauli Murray's ground zero. In 1966, she introduced Friedan to two heavy hitting and seasoned Washington insiders: Catherine East, executive director of the Citizens Advisory Council and Mary Eastwood, a Justice Department lawyer, and the ad hoc organization began looking into the hundreds of thousands of EEOC women's discrimination complaints that were being patently ignored. Friedan instantly recognized this was the place where feminist action was most needed and could be most transformative. 'I knew now that 'jobs' were the issue for women. I tracked down Pauli Murray at Yale... And I started down the road that would lead to the women's movement.' (Friedan 2000)

East invited Friedan to the Third National Conference of Commissions on the Status of Women (1966) in hopes of protesting the categorization of 'Help Wanted' employment ads as 'male' or 'female' (resulting in all the good jobs being designated for men), and demanding that all EEOC complaints be investigated. When they were refused permission to even address the convention, Friedan and Kay Clarenbach, the Wisconsin commission chair, huddled at their table and, scribbling on yellow paper napkins, wrote into being a new and empowering group: NOW, the National Organization for Women. That night, Friedan invited 15 women to her hotel room to talk through the idea, and met with immediate support. Catherine Conroy (a telephone operator who would later be selected by President Carter to his Advisory Commission for Women) slid a $5 note onto the table and said, 'Put your money down and sign your name'. NOW was born. It was Friedan's creation, as was its mission statement: 'To take the actions needed to bring women into the mainstream of American society – now, full equality for women, in fully equal partnership with men.' (Friedan 1976)

> *'The words were a reflection of Friedan – her impatience; her urge to act; her need for men; her passion for justice.'* (Hennessee 1999)

NOW Means Now!

NOW became the match lighting the new feminist flame, and Friedan was president and chief flamethrower. 'NOW's founders had created an organization before there was a women's movement' (Hennessee 1999) but Friedan remembers a more

Fig. 7 NOW organizers Ms. Billington, Betty Friedan (founder and co-chair) lobbyist Barbara Ireton and lawyer Marguerite Rawalt, 1968.

portentous clarion call: 'we were accepting the challenge history was giving us to take up that unfinished revolution for women's equality that the suffragists had carried forward' (Friedan 2000). The timing was fortuitous, with liberation movements springing up all over America: Caesar Chavez, SDS, SNCC, The Black Panthers, Anti-war crusades. And now women were doing it, too – for themselves. 'It was an era of social change, revealing the power of ordinary people to organize and make demands and reshape society. It all seemed very possible.' (Friedan 2000)

In a very short space of time, NOW was off and running, albeit without a staff, a budget, or offices. The original 300 high-powered and devoted charter members were all volunteers and dues were a mere $5 a year, but they were fiercely committed to gaining equality for women in the economy. However, full equality for women was a long way off. In 1966, the 46 per cent of American women who did work earned about 60 cents for every dollar earned by men, and half of all full-time women workers earned less than $3,690 a year ($29,000 in today's dollars). Women accounted for less than one per cent of federal judges, four percent of all lawyers, and seven per cent of all doctors. The mystique was not only affecting women in their homes – it was also used as justification for locking women out of the better-paid jobs. Sex discrimination was as much a part of the American workplace as the typewriter.

Friedan announced to the new women of NOW that they were going to do something about it. 'Women needed a movement to break through the visible and invisible barriers they faced' (Friedan 2000) and she was determined both to make the barriers visible and strike them down. 'Actions, not just talk,' she promised (Friedan 2000). And she delivered.

Taking it to the Streets

Under the aegis of NOW, women's issues flared into the American consciousness in courtrooms, protests, rallies and media-savvy events. In protesting against sex-segregated help-wanted ads, audacious black lawyer and NOW member Florynce Kennedy (who went by the name of Flo) pronounced to an aghast press, 'Very few jobs actually require either a penis or a vagina.' NY-NOW produced ads with a man in rolled-up pants and the headline: 'Hire him, he's got great legs.' Stewardesses sued to prevent airlines from firing them if they got married, pregnant, or had the audacity to turn 30 – and in 1968, they won.

NOW advocated for women on welfare to get job training and

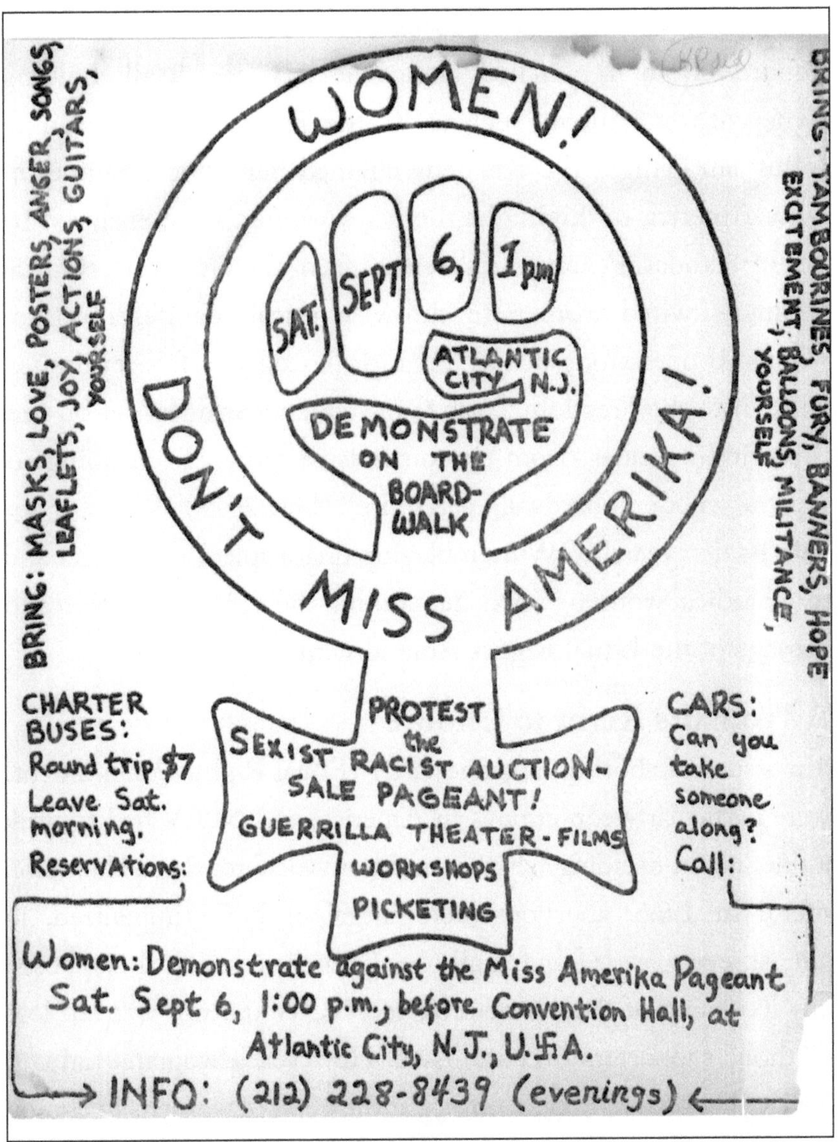

Fig. 8 Poster for the Miss America contest 1968, written by Robin Morgan (© Robin Morgan)

child care, and helped pass laws penalizing federal contractors who discriminated against women, leading to the creation of the first affirmation action programs. The Miss America pageant in Atlantic City became a focus for women's protests: several hundred women marched along the city boardwalk holding signs with statements such as 'Cattle parades are demeaning to human beings'. Flo Kennedy chained herself to a puppet of Miss America to 'highlight the ways women were enslaved by beauty standards', and a press release from the New York Radical Women invited women to throw 'physical manifestations of women's oppression, such as "bras, girdles, curlers, false eyelashes, wigs"' into the Freedom Trash Can (which was never set on fire, following a request from city officials to refrain from doing so, lest the wooden boardwalk catch fire). (Gay 2018)

In its first year, NOW membership quadrupled, as younger and more radical women joined, demanding the right to abortion and passage of the Equal Rights Amendment.

A Woman's Right to Choose

The issues of abortion and the ERA (Equal Rights Amendment) were particularly contentious in America, and NOW had to walk a fine line in deciding whether and how vociferously to champion them. In 1966, abortions were illegal, if not criminalized, in almost every state. The Catholic Church vehemently opposed any loosening of those strictures, and NOW did not want to lose Catholic supporters over the issue. However, a woman's right to control her own reproduction was at the heart of women's liberation and equality, and Friedan insisted NOW take a stand. 'You couldn't have woman's equality without her own control of the reproductive process,' Friedan stated, despite her own ideological misgivings. 'Motherhood is a value to me, and...abortion is not. But the issue had to be confronted.' (Friedan 2000)

'Confrontation' is the gentlest possible way to describe the fight over abortion rights. Hysterical men carrying photos of bloody foetuses screamed 'You murderers!' at young women in overalls screaming back 'Die, sexist pigs!' The violence, shootings and threats, however, were mostly one-way and aimed directly at abortion providers and recipients. Today, the abortion fight in the USA continues unabated, but in the 1960s, the word was hardly spoken until NOW placed the right to a safe and legal abortion into its Bill of Rights and deliberately linked the issue with women's liberation and a woman's right to choose. After the declaration, Friedan's speeches were often interrupted by bomb threats and malevolent protestors. She routinely received death threats by mail. A pro-life activist once pushed a dead foetus in her face. But she never backed down or backed off speaking out about a woman's right to choose motherhood – or not.

Still, women were far from in control, even of their own uterus. The 1873 federal Comstock Law prohibited the production or publication of mere information about birth control (or abortion, or venereal disease). It was not struck down until 1965, and then only married people were granted access to contraceptives. In 1969, Friedan joined Larry Lader as co-founder of NARAL (the National Association for the Repeal of Abortion Laws) and pushed the topic from the shadowy corners into the spotlight. In 1970, Friedan insisted that NOW lobby for New York to become the first state to remove all restrictions on abortion until 24 weeks of pregnancy, and when the bill passed, she was there in the chamber, which she describes as 'packed with the women who had marched and lobbied for the fundamental right to control their own bodies' (Friedan 2000).

In 1972, a woman's right to obtain an abortion in America still varied wildly from state to state, with individual states each passing their own laws, restrictions and prohibitions. In 30 states, all abortions were prohibited; in 16, abortion was banned except in cases of rape, incest or a health threat to the mother; 3 states allowed only residents to obtain an abortion, and New York was the only state to allow abortions legally when sought. NOW and NARAL organized, protested, lobbied and advocated for the Supreme Court to guarantee a woman's constitutional right to choose to terminate a pregnancy. And then, surprisingly, it happened. In January 1973, the historic Supreme Court decision Roe v. Wade swept aside the states' patchwork quilt of laws and legalized abortion, 'guaranteeing women the constitutional right to privacy in determining the outcome of their own pregnancies' (Friedan 2000). Friedan was invited to be in the court that day to watch history happen.

The Brief Life of the ERA

The Equal Rights Amendment was NOW's other great cause, but that outcome wasn't so rapidly or successfully achieved. At first glance, the amendment seems almost impervious to opposition, simply stating: 'Equality of rights under the law shall not be denied by the United States or any state on account of sex.' And yet, the ERA initially faced stiff resistance from labour unions, who wanted to keep in place the 'protective' laws that, in different states, restricted the number of hours a woman could work or the amount of weight she could lift. As a long-time labour advocate, Friedan came to believe that these laws protecting women were actually preventing them from getting overtime pay or being promoted. She also realized that a constitutional amendment was the only way for women's equality to be guaranteed (a view she shares with Supreme Court Justice Ruth Bader Ginsberg, who in 2014 said the one amendment she'd like to see added to the Constitution is the ERA, declaring unequivocally that women and men are persons of equal stature before the law). Friedan noted that:

> *'Title VII had proven a potent weapon for fighting sex discrimination in employment and public accommodations... but it was a law, and a law could be changed or repealed. What you needed to ensure equal opportunity ...was the constitutional end of sex discrimination.'* (Friedan 2000)

The early feminists had tried to get the ERA passed, beginning in 1923, but it wasn't until Martha Griffiths (again!) brought up the amendment in 1971 that it was approved by the House of Representatives. In 1972, the ERA was approved by the Senate. The amendment then required the approval of 38 state legislatures to become embedded in the Constitution. By 1977, it had gained 35 ratifications and with just 3 more states needed, the ERA seemed an inevitability. Both political parties supported the amendment, both houses of Congress, as well as bipartisan Presidents & First Ladies Richard and Pat Nixon, Gerald and Betty Ford, and Jimmy and Rosalyn Carter. Then Phyllis Schlafly showed up.

The Schlafly Effect

Toting baskets of warm muffins (emblazoned with homey, red-chequered tags reading 'To the Breadwinners from the

Bread-Makers'), this helmet-haired, Harvard Law School graduate, Catholic, author, mother of six, radio show host, writer, lobbyist, and head of the right-wing Eagle Forum was the voice of reaction. Schlafly was also Friedan's energy twin, a whirling dervish of vitriol railing against women's liberation, against women working outside the home, against the quite-possibly lesbian 'libs' and against the 'dire' effects of the Equal Rights Amendment (women would be drafted, lose alimony and custody of their children, and be forced to share unisex toilets with hairy men, she warned). In effect, she gave voice to all those women who were threatened to the core by feminism, to men who liked their little women at home, and to the legion of corporate interests whose profits very much depended on docile, appliance-buying housewives and low-paid female workers.

Fig. 9 Phyllis Schlafly demonstrating against the Equal Rights Amendment, 1977.

Throughout the waning 1970s, Schlafly was everywhere at once, delighting conservatives with her rigid stance on family values and strictly defined gender roles, and against feminism, the women's movement, and Betty Friedan in particular. She fired up the forces on the conservative right with fearful predictions of Biblical retribution and caramel-soft recollections of the good old days when men were men and women were underfoot.

> *'Of all the demands of the movement, only two, the ERA and abortion rights, granted women autonomy, legally and personally, challenging the hidden premises, the unspoken prejudices and unexamined dogmas, that ruled society. These two issues served as a rallying point for the reaction...consolidating the power that would culminate in the election of Ronald Reagan in 1980.'* (Hennessee 1999)

The rise of Ronald and Nancy Reagan (a former classmate of Friedan's at Smith) spelled the end of the ERA. The social climate in post-Vietnam America had changed, swinging back to a proudly heterosexual embrace of traditional values which Schlafly ardently championed. By 1982, even with a five-year extension, the ERA remained stalled three states short of ratification and was, for all intents and purposes, dead. (America is still one of the only developed countries without equal protection for women guaranteed in its constitution.)

The Glory Days of Women's Liberation

But back in the late 1960s, the women's liberation movement, with Friedan at NOW's helm, seemed unstoppable.

> *'In those first few years she had led NOW from victory to victory. The feminists were like a small band of guerrillas who ran around sniping at a target here, a target there, and then watched in amazement as the entire edifice crumbled...The sweep of history was with them.'* (Hennessee 1999)

It wasn't just a river of interest in women's rights, it was a fire hose – but fire hoses can be notoriously difficult to manage. Friedan's four years of leading NOW were, like much of her life, tumultuous, exciting, meaningful and traumatic. While leading the organization, she was also writing her second book, getting divorced from her husband of 22 years, raising her two youngest children, giving speeches around the country: all while trying to grow the movement. Everywhere she went, she encouraged women to join NOW.

> *'Friedan was charismatic...she left a trail of NOW chapters in her wake. Women would come up to her after her speeches and tell her their problems and describe their needs, and she would wave her hand like a wand and say, "Do it!" and they did.'* (Hennessee 1999)

Friedan wasn't afraid to recruit across political lines or ideology: 'I wanted these young radical women in our movement, just as I wanted the Catholic nuns and the League of Women Voters and the members of SNCC and the PTA housewives.' (Friedan 2000).

But the fault lines in the movement, and in Friedan's personality, could not be ignored. In a relatively short space of time, the radical element (particularly the lesbians) in the women's movement turned against her. Friedan had a visceral fear that lesbianism would become conflated with feminism and NOW would lose its focus on equality, getting caught up in sexual politics, class or race warfare, or man-hating rhetoric. As radicals were preaching 'out of the mainstream into the revolution' Friedan felt that mainstream was where the most fish lived, and she wanted to keep the focus on equality for all. It was a deep rift in the movement that Friedan could not and would not transcend.

Sisterhood is Problematical

Hennessee (1999) notes that:

> *'the radical women gave the movement its intellectual structure. ...They provided the extremism necessary to revolutions...Women were a class, they argued, oppressed by men. It was a position Friedan could never countenance, and she would fight them to the end on it... They ... invented the slogans that caught fire: 'Sisterhood is Powerful' 'The Personal Is Political.' They introduced the word 'sexism' into the language. Their bible was Beauvoir, not Friedan.'*

At the same time, the NOW board had reached its limit in dealing with Friedan's temper, rudeness, bullying and contempt. She screamed at people on the phone; berated hard- working volunteers; was crude and brusque; alienated friends; created enemies; cursed like a sailor; drank like a pirate, and then became even more hostile and condescending. In a not-exactly repentant mood, she admitted, 'I'm nasty. I'm bitchy. I get mad, but by God, I'm absorbed in what I'm doing' (Cohen 1988).

In the end, Friedan wrestled to hold on to leadership of NOW for four momentous and exhilarating years until 1970, when she decided to step down to avoid a vote she was almost certain to lose to a well-liked and competent black woman, Aileen Hernandez. 'I was just never good enough at that infighting and maneuvering,' Friedan complained later. 'My strengths lay in inspiring and leading the masses and fighting the external enemies. But I was easily outfoxed within the movement and I wasn't so good at fighting for power... it just wasn't worth it.' (Friedan 2000) That wasn't necessarily the way others saw it. 'Friedan's greatest strength—her aggressiveness—is also her greatest weakness,' a fellow NOW member said plaintively (Bohannon 2004).

Friedan's final speech to the NOW board lasted over two hours (a few members went out for dessert after an hour, and came back to find Friedan still talking). She concluded grandiosely with, 'I have led you into history. I leave you now – to make new history.' (Hennessee 1999) On her way out the door, Friedan announced to the press that she was organizing a historic national Women's March to be held on 26 August 1970 to commemorate the 50th anniversary of the ratification of the 19th Amendment. Her thunderbolt came as a complete surprise to NOW's new leadership, which declined to participate or donate its time. The march was a mere four months away.

The Women's March 1970

That first Women's March made history and was perhaps Friedan's finest hour. Over the summer, she and her posse of volunteers raised thousands of dollars for buttons and placards at fancy benefits at estates in the Hamptons, and raised awareness

Fig. 10 Poster for The Women's March, 26 August 1970. Designed by Gary Yanker.

with outrageous stunts like sheathing the Statue of Liberty in a banner reading 'Women of the World, Unite!' They surreptitiously slapped 'This ad insults women' on sexist billboards and advertising all around New York City, and turned City Hall into a riotous day-care centre, as working women brought their children to work to demonstrate the need for childcare. Friedan's vision was to bring together radicals and conservatives, old suffragettes and teenage girls, mothers and daughters in one big, sweeping display of women's unity and power. And true to form, Betty's organizational prowess exceeded all expectations.

At 5pm on 26 August 1970, over 50,000 women in t-shirts, costumes and hats marched down the middle of Fifth Avenue, bringing rush hour to a complete halt. Supporters hung out of museum, office and apartment windows, cheering the marchers on. Photographers captured image after image of the wildly diverse crowd of women carrying banners, hugging, laughing, and marching together to declare their sisterhood. Across America, over 100,000 other activists marched in their own parades in more than 90 cities and small towns in 42 states. NOW's membership climbed to 15,000. And Friedan presided over the entire event; the queen bee of women's liberation – at least for the day. Watching the passion of the women in the streets, Friedan had another one of her 'Aha!' moments, as she realized what her next step must be.

> *'From now on, our thrust will be political,' Friedan told a reporter from the New York Post the day after the march, blithely leapfrogging on to a new arena. 'This was a necessary stage, but that job is over with. From now on, we have no need to stagnate in navel-gazing rap sessions or man-hating... We are going to run.'* (Hennessee 1999)

National Women's Political Caucus

In June 1971, the first meeting of the National Women's Political Caucus brought together four unlikely bedfellows and feminist icons: Betty Friedan, who secretly wanted to run for the US Senate; the newly-elected and extravagantly colourful politico Bella Abzug, who had just been elected to Congress; Shirley Chisholm, the first black congresswoman who would run for President in 1972 under the motto, 'Unbossed and Unbought'; and glamorous feminist cover girl Gloria Steinem, publisher of *Ms.* magazine. NWPC's mission was two-fold: to get women elected to national, state and local office, and to persuade both the Republican and Democratic parties to support passage of the Equal Rights Amendment. Their pithy slogan was, 'Make policy, not coffee'. At the end of the meeting, Friedan went home and immediately fired up her troops. They began by organizing a telephone campaign to every woman activist across America. The organization was to be the first political organization of women in the USA since the suffragettes.

'The NWPC was another NOW, a new call to arms, with Friedan on horseback at the head of the troops.' (Hennessee 1999) She was great at drumming up support among women of every race, colour, class and sexual orientation, but the infighting began almost immediately. At the raucous July 1971 organizing conference of 2,000 women, Friedan and Abzug clashed over whether NWPC would support all mainstream women candidates, or just those who were true reformers. Friedan simply wanted more women in politics, regardless, citing research showing the addition of just two women to a state legislature would 'begin to change the agenda...in terms of legislation affecting life – childcare, health care, senior citizens, even the environment' (Friedan 2000). Friedan's sweet spot had always been to stay as mainstream as possible, unfurling the big tent, while Abzug and Steinem were more radically feminist and deeply attuned to minority and truly progressive candidates. In a bitter rejection, at the end of the conference Steinem was chosen as the NWPC spokesperson (a position Friedan desperately wanted).

NWPC's first big coming-out party was at the Democratic convention in 1972, and it did not go particularly well. Contentious battles erupted within the NWPC ranks over Shirley Chisholm's candidacy for President (and for Vice-President); over how hard to push the abortion plank of the Democratic platform (Friedan had written a masterful draft); over Steinem's role as perpetual media darling (which made almost every other woman somewhat jealous and enraged Friedan); and over how to wrest political power from the men who had always held it. The group of women involved included both political neophytes and seasoned brawlers, and collectively they had far less leverage than they had anticipated. Even though women made up 53 per cent of the electorate and voted at far higher rates than men, in 1972 less than three per cent of Congress was female.

NWPC Triumphs and Tribulations

Despite the disappointment of the 1972 conventions, the caucus was highly effective in realizing its goal of getting women, and women's issues, into the room. NWPC had demanded that 40 per cent of the Democratic delegates to the convention be women – three times the number it had been in 1968. Even at the Republican convention, the number of women delegates was doubled. For the first time, abortion was debated on national television; a woman ran for vice president; and a woman was chosen to chair the Democratic National Committee. And in November, for the first time, five new congresswomen won their races and headed to Washington.

For two years, Friedan travelled far and wide organizing new chapters of the NWPC in Arizona, Iowa, Ohio, Oregon, Missouri and Mississippi, speaking on women's rights and supporting women candidates on behalf of the caucus. So she was quite confident that she would be elected to the national steering committee at the 1973 NWPC national convention. Alas, following a weird and never-resolved confusion that arose over vote tallying, she was not. It was a devastating blow, particularly since it marked the repeated triumph of beautiful blonde Gloria Steinem, who with Bella Abzug would inherit 'Friedan's' organization.

> *'The pattern was always the same. I would start one organization; it would be taken over. I'd start another*

> *organization; it would be taken over...NOW, NARAL, the NWPC—they'd all be taken over...but it wouldn't stop me because people wanted to hear what I had to say... So I sort of figured out that my contribution was going to be offering some vision.'* (Friedan 2000)

1973 would mark the end of Friedan's full participation in the women's movement, though hardly the end of her advocacy. 'What I had to give, I decided, was... to advance women's rights by teaching, lecturing and writing.' (Friedan 2000) And so she did.

Hennessee (1999) notes that the intellectual world from which Friedan 'had so reluctantly torn herself in 1943 was her true home; the exchange of ideas was the thing that excited her most'. This is debatable, as Friedan also seemed to relish power, fame and lavish attention. However, Friedan was undoubtedly passionate about spreading the word, and would go on to teach at Temple, Yale, Mt. Vernon and Harvard. She also lectured around the country to thousands of avid followers and attended conferences, symposia, seminars, and think tanks around the world – all with a focus on feminist issues in society. With her radar for what was coming next, and her skill at keeping herself politically aware, well-connected, and intellectually relevant, she was never far from the spotlight.

Conclusion

Betty Friedan's credentials as a profound feminist influence are indisputable. Her book, *The Feminine Mystique*, is widely acknowledged as the spark that ignited the Second Wave of feminism in America and around the world, inspiring millions of women to change their life, seek out a career, fight for equality and their human rights, and participate more fully in the world. Her polemical arguments laid bare and then undermined the psychological and cultural constructs of male superiority, Freudian theory, and female dependency and weakness. Finally, her activism made her a role model and tireless advocate for progressive causes and women's issues throughout her long life.

Betty Friedan was also a controversial and contradictory personality – larger than life, charismatic, confusing and often maddening. Despite her life's work in advocating for women, on a personal level she didn't find it easy to relate to the female species. Friendships were difficult for her to maintain, she had no compunction about sleeping with other women's husbands, and she desperately craved and adored men's approval. She could be caustic, critical, brutally competitive, cringe-worthy in her vanity, and voracious in her need for attention. In all of this she was not unlike many of her male peers in psychology, such as professors Alfred Kinsey ('fornicate early, fornicate often, fornicate in every possible way') and Timothy Leary ('turn on, tune in, drop out'), whose equally high profiles coincided with multiple infidelities (and drug/drinking problems, in the case of Leary). Even Albert Ellis, father of cognitive therapy, explained people's mental struggles as due to the fact that '...they're screwed up! They're out of their fucking minds! We're all out of our fucking minds!' So perhaps within the world of 1960s psychology, Betty Friedan's seemingly wild behaviours were judged more harshly than the men's because she was a woman, who refused to capitulate to the idea of the feminine mystique.

And yet, despite the self-inflicted wounds of hubris and volatility that caused her to create, cultivate and then be banished from one inspired women's organization after another, Friedan never stopped fighting for the things she believed in. When one door shut in her face (usually with some vigour), she discovered and walked through another – reinventing herself as a teacher, convener of think tanks, international diplomat, and intellectual explorer. Well into her 80s, she found new ways to care deeply about the world and women's place in it, using her piercing intellect and prescient perspective to shine a light on issues as diverse as income inequality, ageism, work/life balance, the ascension of identity politics and the 'angry white male' influence in American culture. Twenty-five years before these topics became part of the national conversation, Betty Friedan was writing about it and talking about it. In a 1992 interview, she said that men were burdened with a masculine mystique: 'Men had to be supermen: stoic, responsible meal tickets. Dominance is a burden. Most men who are honest will admit that.' There is, she said, 'a real need of men to evolve through the burden of the masculine mystique, the burden of machismo'.

Friedan was quintessentially of her time, powerfully bringing to light an ideology that had been unseen, so 'normal' did it appear in terms of behavioural expectations in the 1960s. She articulated the painful reality of women who were soul-sick, trapped in a world that systematically undervalued their strength, intelligence, capabilities and potential, even while it celebrated their fortunate circumstances and 'lucky' lives. (And if this were true of 'lucky' women, how much more difficult must it have been for all women?) Friedan was in other ways miles ahead of her time, anticipating the next big thing and bringing it to reality by the sheer force of her brilliance and relentless perseverance. If you met her you might not like her, but it's unlikely you would ever forget her.

Friedan made things happen. And look at what did happen. In the decade between the February 1963 publication of *The Feminine Mystique* and Roe v. Wade in January 1973, when abortion finally became legal across the USA, 'the essential work was done, the groundwork laid, the nation's consciousness changed' (Hennessee 1999). It was an astonishing accomplishment, commandeered by a small corps of women, and it amazed even Friedan. 'It is a mystery, the whole thing—why it happened, how it started. What gave any of us the courage to make that leap?' (Friedan 1977)

The women's movement may have been like a comet, blazing beautifully across the 1970s sky before it flamed out, but it unleashed a feminist consciousness that has fundamentally changed the lives of women in America.

As of 2019, in the USA:

> *102 women serve in the US House of Representatives.*
>
> *The gender income gap has dropped from 40 per cent to 20 per cent.*
>
> *47 per cent of the American workforce is female.*
>
> *Women make up 57 per cent of college undergraduates and 59 per cent of college masters' degree candidates.*
>
> *45 per cent of all lawyers and 40 per cent of doctors and surgeons are women.*
>
> *40 per cent of American businesses are women-owned.*
>
> *3 of the 9 current Supreme Court justices are women.*

These are compelling statistics, but perhaps more important is the extraordinary change in what women want and expect for themselves. A young American woman today simply cannot imagine a world in which she has no access to birth control, no ability to pursue any career she wants, no pathway to obtain a credit card or mortgage in her own name. The **feminine** mystique seems as outdated and quaint as hair rollers and 8-track tapes – and nothing would have delighted Friedan more.

In 1964, she told an audience in San Francisco:

> *'You...are the new image of women: as person, as heroine. You live actively in society. You are not solely dependent on your husbands and your children for your identity. You do not live your life vicariously through them. You do not wait passively for that wise man to*

make the decisions that will shape your society, but move in and help shape society yourself, and begin to make it a more human world. You bridge that old, obsolete division that splits life into man's world of thought and action and woman's world of love. With little help from society, you have begun to make a new pattern in which marriage, motherhood, homemaking—the traditional roles of women—are merged with the possibility of women as individuals, as decision-makers, as creators of the future.' (Friedan 1976)

With a lifetime of words and work, Friedan willed that woman into being. Well played, Betty.

Bibliography

Bohannon, Lisa Frederiksen (2004) *Woman's Work: The Story of Betty Friedan*, North Carolina: Morgan Reynolds Publishing

Cohen, Marcia (1988) *The Sisterhood*, New York: Simon & Schuster

Eagle, Jennie (2018) 'Betty Friedan and Juliet Mitchell: Critiques of Ideology and Power', *CUNY Academic Works*, https://academicworks.cuny.edu/gc_etds/2480

Flexner, Eleanor (1975) *Century of Struggle: The Woman's Rights Movement in the United States*, Cambridge, Massachusetts: Belknap Press of Harvard University Press

Friedan, Betty (1963) *The Feminine Mystique*, New York: Norton

Friedan, Betty (1976) *It Changed My Life*, New York: Random House

Friedan, Betty (1981) *The Second Stage*, New York: Summit Books, imprint of Simon & Schuster

Friedan, Betty (1993) *The Fountain of Age*, New York: Simon & Schuster

Friedan, Betty (2000) *Life So Far*, New York: Simon & Schuster

Gay, Roxane (2018) 'Fifty Years Ago, Protesters Took on the Miss America Pageant and Electrified the Feminist Movement', *Smithsonian Magazine,* January 2018

Ginsberg, L (2000) 'Ex-hubby fires back at feminist icon Betty', *New York Post*, 5 July 2000

Groopman, Jerome (2019) 'Medicine in Mind', *The New Yorker*, 27 May 2019

Hennessee, Judith (1999) *Betty Friedan: Her Life*, New York: Random House

Hole, Judith and Ellen Levine (1971) *Rebirth of Feminism*, New York: Quadrangle Books

Horowitz, David (2000) *Betty Friedan and the Making of The Feminine Mystique*, Massachusetts: University of Massachusetts Press

TIME magazine (1976) 'Women of the Year: Great Changes, New Chances, Tough Choices', 5 January 1976

Biography

Betty Londergan began her writing career in journalism, spent most of her working life as a Creative Director in advertising, then went on to write two books on motherhood: *I'm too Sexy for my Volvo*, and *The Agony and the Agony*. She created two year-long blogging projects: *What Gives 365*, giving away $100 a day to causes she felt were making the world a better place, and *Heifer 12x12*, travelling to 18 countries in 12 months with Heifer International. Betty lives in Atlanta with her husband.

Acknowledgements

I'd like to thank Sarah Tomley for bringing me this project and letting me choose Betty Friedan to write about, as well as editing and shaping the book. I'd also like to thank my mother for her example of a strong determined woman who isn't afraid to fight for what she believes in. We didn't end up believing in the same things, but she was my hero.

Picture Credits

Fig 1. 'Betty Friedan 1960 ' by Fred Palumbo, World Telegram staff photographer. Restored by Adam Cuerden (https://commons.wikimedia.org/wiki/File:Betty Friedan 1960.jpg). Marked as public domain, more details on Wikimedia Commons: https://commons.wikimedia.org/wiki/Template:Library of Congress – no known copyright restrictions . Fig 2. The Feminine Mystique, 1963 edition. Published by W.W. Norton & Co. Fig 3. 'The Kanizsa Triangle'. Fibonacci (https://commons.wikimedia.org/wiki/File:Kanizsa triangle.svg), 'Kanizsa triangle', https://creativecommons.org/licenses/by-sa/3.0/legalcode. Fig 4. 'The Rubin Vase.' user:mikkalai (https://commons.wikimedia.org/wiki/File:Facevase.JPG). 'Facevase', faces by Bowden & Brazil, https://creativecommons.org/publicdomain/zero/1.0/legalcode. Fig 5. Vintage Ad (Flickr.Jamie) from Maclean's, 26 March 1960. Creative Commons license (CC by 2.0). Fig 6. 'Suffragettes on way to Boston (LOC).' Library of Congress, Prints and Photographs Division. Image c.1910.. No known copyright restrictions. Fig 7. NOW organizers. Unknown (https://commons.wikimedia.org/wiki/File:NOW women.jpg), 'NOW women', marked as public domain, more details on Wikimedia Commons: https://commons.wikimedia.org/wiki/Template:SIA-no known copyright restrictions. Fig 8. Poster for Miss America contest, 1968. Robin MorganPapers, David M. Rubenstein Rare Book & Manuscript Library, Duke University. Copyright Robin Morgan; used with permission. Fig 9. Warren K. Leffler (https://commons.wikimedia.org/wiki/File:Activist Phyllis Schafly wearing a "Stop ERA" badge, demonstrating with other women against the Equal Rights Amendment in front of the White House, Washington, D.C. (42219314092).jpg), 'Activist Phyllis Schafly wearing a "Stop ERA" badge, demonstrating with other women against the Equal Rights Amendment in front of the White House, Washington, D.C. (42219314092)', https://creativecommons.org/publicdomain/zero/1.0/legalcode Fig. 10 Yanker Poster Collection (https://commons.wikimedia.org/wiki/File:Women's Strike, August 26 LCCN2015648058.jpg), 'Women's Strike, August 26 LCCN2015648058', marked as public domain, more details on Wikimedia Commons: https://commons.wikimedia.org/wiki/Template:PD-US

This exciting new series of books sets out to explore the life and theories of the world's leading intellectuals in a clear and understandable way. The series currently includes the following subject areas:

Art History
Psychology
Philosophy
Sociology
Politics

For more information about forthcoming titles in the Who the Hell is...? series, go to **www.whothehellis.co.uk**

If any of our readers would like to put in a request for a particular intellectual to be included in our series, then please contact us at **into@whothehellis.co.uk**

www.ingramcontent.com/pod-product-compliance
Ingram Content Group UK Ltd.
Pitfield, Milton Keynes, MK11 3LW, UK
UKHW041640190726
13854UKWH00006B/2602